C I T Y P A C K
Boston

By Sue Gordon

Fodor's

Fodor's Travel Publications, Inc.
New York • Toronto • London • Sydney • Auckland

WWW.FODORS.COM/

Contents

Life **5 – 12**

How to organize your time **13 – 22**

Top 25 sights **23 – 48**

About this book

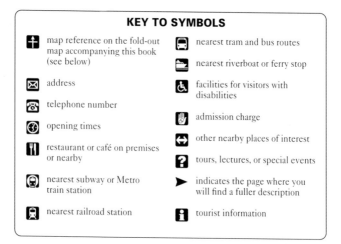

KEY TO SYMBOLS

🕂 map reference on the fold-out
  map accompanying this book
  (see below)

⊠ address

☎ telephone number

🕓 opening times

🍴 restaurant or café on premises
  or nearby

🚇 nearest subway or Metro
  train station

🚆 nearest railroad station

🚌 nearest tram and bus routes

⛴ nearest riverboat or ferry stop

♿ facilities for visitors with
  disabilities

✋ admission charge

↔ other nearby places of interest

❓ tours, lectures, or special events

▶ indicates the page where you
  will find a fuller description

ℹ tourist information

Citypack Boston is divided into six sections to cover the six most important aspects of your visit to Boston. It includes:

- An introduction to the city and its people
- Itineraries, walks and excursions
- The top 25 sights to visit—as selected by the author
- Features about different aspects of the city that make it special
- Detailed listings of restaurants, hotels, shops, and nightlife
- Practical information

In addition, easy-to-read side panels provide fascinating extra facts and snippets, highlights of places to visit and invaluable practical advice.

CROSS-REFERENCES

To help you make the most of your visit, cross-references, indicated by ▶, show you where to find additional information about a place or subject.

MAPS

- **The fold-out map** in the wallet at the back of the book is a comprehensive street plan of Boston. All the map references given in the book refer to this map. For example, Trinity Church on Copley Square has the following information:
🕂 F5—indicating the grid square of the map in which Trinity Church will be found.

- **The city map** found on the inside front and back covers of the book itself is for quick reference. It shows the Top 25 Sights in the city, described on pages 24–48, which are clearly plotted by number (🮱 – 🮲 , not page number) from west to east.

PRICES

Where appropriate, an indication of the cost of an establishment is given by **$** signs: **$$$** denotes higher prices, **$$** denotes average prices, while **$** denotes lower charges. An indication of the admission charge (for all museums and galleries) is given by categorizing the standard adult rate as follows: Expensive (over $7), Moderate ($4–$6) and Cheap (under $4).

BOSTON
life

INTRODUCING BOSTON

You may well reflect on the wisdom of those early British colonists who escaped to a new life in Boston. Of course it has changed in size and, radically, in shape since the 1620s, but it is still a place blessed in its location, with the sea and all its pleasures lapping at the front door, the sweeping Charles River at the side entrance, and forests and mountains in its backyard.

But what of the city itself? Its history—and there simply is no other American city that has such a long history—is deeply revered and meticulously preserved. Its role as the cradle of the nation and the birthplace of the American Revolution is vividly interpreted in various landmarks along the Freedom Trail, a red line on the sidewalk that guides you from one significant site to the next. In the 19th century wealthy Bostonians (and there were many) traveled extensively in Europe, leaving their city an exceptional cultural legacy that is now displayed in such nationally and internationally important treasure-houses as the Museum of Fine Arts, the Isabella Stewart Gardner Museum, and Harvard University's Fogg Museum.

As for the architecture, one of the most exciting things about Boston are the unexpected juxtapositions of elegant old and high-rise new, not least I. M. Pei's gleaming shaft of glass, the Hancock Tower, which at every turn, it seems, rises serene above Victorian brownstone rooftops. Musically, the city is home not only to the world-class Boston Symphony Orchestra, but also the Boston Pops, seriously good jazz, and some hip rock bands. The malls, designer boutiques, and antiques stores offer good shopping, too.

Boston may have one eye gazing at the past, but the other is firmly fixed on the future. Just across the river is Cambridge, home of Harvard and M.I.T., and between them Boston and Cambridge boast over 60 colleges

The Proper Bostonian

The Brahmins, or Proper Bostonians, trace their origins to the wealthy merchants of the 18th and 19th centuries. Membership of these families—names such as Lowell, Appleton, Cabot—may now be comparatively minimal, but their influence is still felt.

"And this is the city of Boston
The land of the bean and the cod
Where the Lowells talk only to
Cabots
And the Cabots talk only to God."
Toast made by James
Collins Bassidy, Alumni
dinner at Holy Cross
College, 1910

Charles Street storefront

and universities. Not surprisingly, life in "the Hub" has a certain intellectual edge. The 100,000 students give the place a buzz. The international students among them, together with the city's ethnic population, add a certain diversity, which is reflected in the wide range of cuisines on offer in a cornucopia of restaurants.

Trinity Church reflected in the glass of the Hancock Tower

7

Americans used to think of Bostonians as snobby, sedate, a little behind the times—a legacy of the Brahmins, as the city's rich and powerful upper-caste establishment was termed in the 19th century. On élitist Beacon Hill, you may get a sense of what that was all about. More to the point, the city is now not only one of the most attractive in the country but also one of the easiest to explore. A day or two's easy footwork will cover the compact, historic core. With the airport just across the harbor, whether you are doing the sights or attending a conference, you will probably spend the visit unaware of any burgeoning suburban development. If you do tire of walking, want to conserve energy for the Fenway galleries or plan to venture over the river to Harvard Square in Cambridge, there is always the T, as the subway is called, which is cheap, clean, efficient, and simple to use.

Al fresco *dining on Newbury Street*

The Big Dig

Boston's one major blight currently is the "Big Dig", an epic roadworks project that will take until 2004 to put below ground the horrendous expressway, the Central Artery. Once buried, it will be covered with parkland, reuniting with downtown Boston the North End and the Waterfront that currently can only be reached by diving beneath the so-called Green Monster.

And what is it like, living in Boston? In the city of high-rise finance and high-tech research, the city of the Red Sox and the Celtics, Filene's Basement and Dunkin' Donuts, Italian *feste* and Irish politicians (Democrat or Democrat?) Bostonians work hard, but they also play hard. If you are up early, you'll see downtown professionals hustling along in their sneakers and sharp suits, styrofoam cup of coffee in one hand, a bagel in a bag in the other. Supper is eaten early, and then there's the evening entertainment—maybe a game at Fenway Park (you never know, the Red Sox just might make it this season), a concert at Symphony Hall, a foreign film, a meal in a sushi bar. Saturday sees many Bostonians shopping in the North End's Italian groceries, jogging on the Esplanade, or on a visit to the Aquarium. Sundays could mean a stroll through Back Bay Fens, brunch and an afternoon concert at the Gardner Museum, or perhaps the family might head for one of the Boston Harbor Islands for the day. For vacations, there may be a trip to Maine or Cape Cod, and in winter there's skiing in the Berkshires, Vermont, or New Hampshire. There is so much choice for Bostonians. Their forebears chose well.

BOSTON IN FIGURES

POPULATION
- 1690: 7,000
- 1790: 18,320
- 1825: 58,277
- 1850: 136,881
- 1875: 341,919
- 1996: 574,283

TOPOGRAPHY
- Area of central Boston: 48.6 square miles
- 58 percent is landfill, including Back Bay, South End, South Boston
- 43 miles of waterfront
- Beacon Hill was one of three peaks called Trimountaine by early colonists

NICKNAMES
- The Hub: in 1858 Oliver Wendell Holmes, essayist and lecturer, called the Massachusetts State House "the hub of the solar system"; now applied to Boston as a whole
- Beantown: as it was against the law for the Puritans to cook on Sunday, they prepared baked beans on Saturdays. This custom earned Boston the nickname Beantown
- Athens of America: expression used by William Tudor in 1819
- Brahmin: term coined by Oliver Wendell Holmes after the high-ranking Hindu caste
- Proper Bostonians (▶ 6)
- "Old Ironsides": U.S.S. *Constitution*, because her wooden hull survived many attacks
- The T: rapid transport system (subway)

BOSTON & CAMBRIDGE ACADEMIA
- 67 colleges and universities
- 100,000 students
- 8 major medical research centers
- Half the population of Cambridge is connected with academic institutions

BOSTON FIRSTS
- Boston Common, first park in U.S.: 1634
- *Boston News Letter*, first newspaper in U.S.: 1704
- Alexander Graham Bell makes first telephone call: 1875
- The first subway in the Western hemisphere opens under Boston Common: 1897
- First kidney transplant: 1954

A CHRONOLOGY

Pre-1620	The Boston area is inhabited by the Massachusetts Algonquins.
1620	Pilgrims arrive on *Mayflower* and establish first English colony in Plymouth.
1624	Clergyman William Blaxton settles on what is now Beacon Hill on the Shawmut peninsula.
1629	Puritans found Massachusetts Bay Colony in Charlestown.
1630	John Winthrop becomes first governor and Colony moves to Shawmut peninsula.
1636	Harvard College is founded to train ministers.
1680	The house that Paul Revere was to live in a century later is built. Most of Boston is concentrated in what is to become the North End, around the flourishing seaport.
1760s	Britain imposes a series of tax-levying acts. Colonists protest at having to pay taxes when they have no representation in government. Tension mounts. Patriots are led by "Sons of Freedom" Sam Adams and John Hancock.
1770	March 5: British soldiers kill five colonists outside the State House ("Boston Massacre").
1773	December 16: Patriots protest at the Tea Act by throwing tea into the sea (Boston Tea Party).
1775	The Revolution starts in Boston.
1776	March 17: British leave Boston July 18: Declaration of Independence read from State House balcony.
1799–1805	Beacon Hill is pared down by some 60ft.
1790s	China trade prosperity.
1795	Architect Charles Bulfinch (➤ 12) starts new State House.

1800	The Mount Vernon Proprietors (including Bulfinch) develop Beacon Hill.
1826	Mayor Josiah Quincy extends waterfront and builds Quincy Market.
1840s	Irish immigrants, fleeing the Potato Famine, pour into the North End.
1856	Work begins on filling in and developing the Back Bay as a new residential area for the élite.
1877	Swan boats come to the Public Garden.
1880s	Irish make their mark in politics; Irish mayors include John F. Fitzgerald ("Honey-Fitz"), grandfather of John F. Kennedy, and the charismatic James Curley.
1895	Frederick Law Olmsted, Boston's first landscape architect, designs an interconnecting chain of parks, "The Emerald Necklace".
1897	First Boston Marathon takes place.
1918	Red Sox win the World Series—their first and only victory.
1928	Boston Garden opened. It closed on September 29, 1995, the last game being played on September 26, 1995.
1957	First of 16 NBA championship victories by the Celtics.
1960	JFK elected President.
1960s–1970s	An extensive urban renewal program includes I. M. Pei's office building John Hancock Tower.
1989	Work begins on burying the Central Artery (► 8).
1990	Art heist at the Gardner.
1997	U.S.S. *Constitution* celebrates 200th birthday.

11

PEOPLE & EVENTS FROM HISTORY

Tea is thrown overboard in protest against the British tax on tea—a significant event in the build-up to revolution

Charles Bulfinch

It is often said that Charles Bulfinch (1763–1844) more or less made Boston architecturally. Returning from a trip to Europe, he designed a new State House and a dozen churches. He then turned to the large-scale residential development of Beacon Hill. His neoclassical style became known as "Federal." Having made his mark in Boston, Bulfinch went on to design the Capitol in Washington, D.C.

THE BOSTON TEA PARTY

By the mid-1700s the New England colonists were feeling increasingly angry at British interference in their lucrative seafaring trade. In 1773 the Tea Act not only levied a tax but gave London's East India Company a monopoly on the tea trade. Tension mounted and, in December, patriots took decisive action by boarding three of the company's ships in the harbor and dumping the tea overboard. The British retaliated by besieging Boston, and war became inevitable.

PAUL REVERE'S RIDE

In his lifetime Revere (1735–1818) was known principally as a silversmith. He was also involved in the pre-Revolutionary activities of the "Sons of Liberty" and acted as a messenger to warn local militia men about British military preparations. On the night of April 18, 1775, as a signal to patriots in Charlestown that the troops were leaving, he arranged for lanterns to be hung in the steeple of Old North Church. He then left for Concord himself but, with William Dawes and Sam Prescott, was captured by the British. Only Prescott escaped. Most press reports did not even mention Revere by name. However, in 1861 Longfellow was inspired to pen a poem. He used poetic license: Revere receives rather than gives the signal; Revere not only rides to Concord alone, he arrives safely. And thus, Revere the folk hero is immortalized.

J. F. K.

John Fitzgerald Kennedy was born in the Boston suburb of Brookline on May 29, 1917 into a politically active Irish-American family. A Harvard graduate, he served in the navy in World War II and in 1946 was elected to Congress from Boston. From 1953 to 1960 he served in the U.S. Senate. He was elected president in 1960. Good-looking and charismatic, with a beautiful and equally charismatic wife, he was a symbol of the nation's hopes for a progressive future. Tragically, on November 22, 1963, he was assassinated in Dallas.

BOSTON
how to organize your time

13

ITINERARIES

ITINERARY ONE	ON AND OFF THE FREEDOM TRAIL
Morning	Massachusetts State House (➤ 38). Bowdoin Street, Derne Street, Hancock Street to Harrison Gray Otis House (➤ 37). Cambridge Street, Bowdoin Street, Beacon Street to Boston Athenaeum (➤ 39).
Lunch	Black Goose, opposite Athenaeum.
Afternoon	Park Street, then Tremont Street for Old Granary Burying Ground (➤ 56) and King's Chapel (➤ 56.) Keep on trail to Old South Meeting House (➤ 40), Old State House (➤ 41), and Faneuil Hall (➤ 42). Refreshment in Faneuil Hall Marketplace. Continue on trail to Paul Revere House (➤ 45) and Old North Church, North End (➤ 44). If time, U.S.S. *Constitution* (➤ 43).
ITINERARY TWO	BEACON HILL & BACK BAY
Morning	Start at Park T. Walk up Park Street and left down Beacon Street. Right onto Charles Street to explore Beacon Hill (➤ 16, 35) Coffee on Charles Street. Try Rebecca's Bakery. Public Garden (➤ 36) to Washington Statue and onto Commonwealth Avenue (➤ 33). Left onto Exeter Street to Boylston Street.
Lunch	Samuel Adams Brewhouse, 710 Boylston Street, then left out of Brewhouse along Boylston to Prudential Center.
Afternoon	Walk through Prudential Center to Christian Science Center for Mapparium (➤ 29). Return through Prudential Center and covered walk to Copley Place. Exit onto Dartmouth Street. Copley Square for Boston Public Library (➤ 31) and Trinity Church (➤ 32). Tea in the Copley Plaza Hotel.
Evening	John Hancock Tower Observatory (➤ 30). Meal in Newbury Street.

ITINERARY THREE	**CULTURE IN FENWAY**
Morning	T to the Museum of Fine Arts (➤ 28), taking refreshment when necessary in the Galleria Café.
Lunch	Around the corner in Isabella Stewart Gardner Museum Café.
Afternoon	Isabella Stewart Gardner Museum. Through Back Bay Fens to Boylston Street.
Evening	Drink or meal at Sonsie, Newbury Street. Prudential Skywalk (➤ 30).
ITINERARY FOUR	**CAMBRIDGE**
Morning	Take the T to Harvard Square for coffee With Harvard Coop on your left and the news-stand on your right, walk up Mass. Ave. to the First Church Burial Ground. Cross Mass. Ave. and Peabody Street to enter Harvard Yard (➤ 25). Walk through to Quincy Street for the Fogg Art Museum and Busch-Reisinger (➤ 26). Follow Quincy Street to Sackler Museum (➤ 26). If you wish to see the Glass Flowers (➤ 26), continue on Quincy Street across Cambridge Street. Left on Kirkland Street, right onto Oxford Street. Retrace steps to corner of Oxford and Kirkland streets and return through Harvard Yard to Harvard Square.
Lunch	Choice in Brattle Street.
Afternoon	Continue westward on Brattle Street. Opposite American Repertory Theatre, divert right to see Radcliffe Yard (➤ 25). Brattle Street to Longfellow House (➤ 24). Walk through the park in front of Longfellow House. Turn left on Mt. Auburn Street to return to Harvard Square .
Evening	Grendel's Den (➤ 67) or House of Blues (➤ 68)

15

WALKS

Louisburg Square

THE SIGHTS

- Beacon Hill (➤ 35)
- Nichols House (➤ 53)
- African Meeting House (➤ 53)

INFORMATION

Distance 1½ miles
Time 1 hour
Start point Beacon Street (by State House)
⊞ bIV/B4
🚇 Park
End point Beacon Street at Charles Street
⊞ bIV/B4
🚇 Park

BEACON HILL

Beacon Hill is steep in parts and some of the streets are cobbled. Wear suitable shoes.

Start on Beacon Street at the State House and walk down hill. The Appleton Mansions at No. 39, where poet Longfellow was married, and No. 40 have some of the highly prized purple panes (flawed originals that are now rare, ➤ 35). At the bottom turn right onto Charles Street, up Chestnut Street and left onto Willow Street. On the left is a much-photographed view down Acorn Street. Houses in lanes such as this were for servants. Continue to Mt. Vernon Street. The beautiful Louisburg Square, where Louisa May Alcott died, is ahead. Continue up Mt. Vernon Street and detour onto Walnut Street and briefly into Chestnut to see Nos. 13, 15, and 17, a lovely trio. Return to Mt. Vernon Street to visit the Nichols House, a family home until the 1960s. At the end of Mt. Vernon, turn left onto Joy Street. Smith Court, important in the history of blacks in Boston, is farther down Joy Street, over Pinckney Street. Turn onto Pinckney Street, with its fine view of the Charles River. Detour right onto Anderson Street and right again onto Revere Street. Between 29 and 25 the columned façade is a *trompe l'oeil*. Return to Pinckney and follow it down to Charles Street.

Return to Beacon Street. From here you can join the Freedom Trail.

THE FREEDOM TRAIL TO COPP'S HILL

The Freedom Trail is a long-established walking tour that links all the most significant sites from Boston's colonial and revolutionary era. A red line on the sidewalk makes it easy to follow.

Start at the information center on Boston Common. Head for the classical gold-domed Massachusetts State House. Facing it is the Shaw Monument. Come down Park Street to "Brimstone Corner" (gunpowder was stored in Park Street Church in the war of 1812) and turn left onto Tremont Street. Many famous people are buried in the Old Granary Burying Ground. Cross to King's Chapel, the oldest church site in Boston still in use. Turn down School Street. A sidewalk mosaic marks the site of the first free school, open to all. On the left, in front of the Old City Hall, is a statue of Benjamin Franklin. At the end of the street, the Old Corner Bookstore was a meeting place for 19th-century literati. Head diagonally right for Old South Meeting House, where the Boston Tea Party started. Follow the red line along Washington Street to Old State House. A circle of stones in the traffic island on State Street marks the site of the Boston Massacre. Cross State Street onto Congress Street. Faneuil Hall and Marketplace (plenty of eating places here) is on the right.

Continue along the trail between the tall glass Holocaust Memorial and the Olde Union Oyster House to Hanover Street. Cross Blackstone Street and follow the walkway under the Expressway to the North End. Turn off Hanover Street onto Richmond Steet for North Square and Paul Revere's House. Back in Hanover Street, turn left onto Revere Mall, passing Revere's statue, with the landmark of Old North Church steeple ahead. Carry on up Hull Street for Copp's Hill Burying Ground.

THE SIGHTS

INFORMATION

Distance 1½ miles
Time 1–4 hours
Start point Boston Common
✚ bIV/B4
🚇 Park
End point Copp's Hill
✚ dI/H3
🚇 North Station

John Hancock's tombstone, Old Granary Burying Ground

EVENING STROLLS

*Faneuil Hall and
Marketplace*

FANEUIL HALL & THE WATERFRONT

For superb views of the city and harbor, start with a drink in the Bay Tower, 60 State Street. Stroll through Faneuil Hall Marketplace, a lively collection of shops and eating places, then follow the Harborwalk across Atlantic Avenue and south along the old wharves of the Waterfront. Cross at Northern Avenue Bridge to enter South Boston. At the far side, look right—up Fort Point Channel—and if you're lucky you will see the Boston Tea Party Ship, a replica of one of the original ships, silhouetted against the evening sky. Finish off with a meal in one of the seafood restaurants in the vicinity.

THE CHARLES RIVER & BACK BAY

From the western edge of the charming Public Garden (on the corner of Commonwealth Avenue and Arlington Street) take Commonwealth Avenue to Dartmouth Street. Turn right and take a footbridge that leads you to the Esplanade. Walk left past pretty Storrow Lagoon to a footbridge onto Fairfield Street. Turn left to reach Commonwealth or Newbury Street and return to Dartmouth Street. Turn right onto Copley Square. Have a drink in the Copley Plaza Hotel, noting the sumptuous décor, then visit the Hancock Tower Observatory for magical night-time views before or after eating at Skipjack's or (for a treat) Café Budapest.

HARVARD SQUARE

Harvard Square is awake till the small hours. The stores are open late and there are plenty of bars, restaurants, and clubs. Stroll around the streets imbibing the atmosphere (or, if you are a book lover, just browse to your heart's content), then retreat to the Charles Hotel's Regatta Bar Jazz Club.

INFORMATION

Faneuil Hall & the Waterfront
Distance 1¼–1½ miles
Time 40 minutes
Start point 60 State Street
🚇 dIII/H4
Ⓜ State
End point Northern Avenue Bridge
🚇 H5
Ⓜ South Station

Charles River & Back Bay
Distance 1¼ miles
Time 30–40 minutes
Start point Public Garden
🚇 F5
Ⓜ Arlington
End point Copley Square
🚇 F5
Ⓜ Copley

Harvard Square
Start/end point Harvard Square
🚇 C2
Ⓜ Harvard Square

ORGANIZED SIGHTSEEING

ON FOOT
Black Heritage Trail ✉ Museum of Afro-American History, 46 Joy Street ☎ 742-1854 Explores the history of the African-American community on Beacon Hill. Guided or self-guided.
Boston by Foot ✉ 77 North Washington Street ☎ 367-2345 Range of tours (May–Oct) including, for children, "Boston by Little Feet".
Freedom Trail ✉ Visitor Center, 15 State Street ☎ 242-5642 Ranger-led tours of the trail that connects Boston's historic sites (➤ 17) (🎟 Free 🕐 Daily spring to fall).

TROLLEY TOURS
All do narrated tours, stopping at major sites, plus principal hotels. One all-day ticket; hop on and off where you like. All year daily from 9AM.
Beantown Trolley (red) ☎ 236-2148 Standard tour takes in Museum of Fine Arts. Also Cambridge tour.
Minute Man Trolley Tours (blue) ☎ 876-5539 **Old Town Trolleys** (green and orange) ☎ 269-7010 Also "Discover Cambridge" and "J.F.K.'s Boston".

DUCK TOURS
Boston Duck Tours ☎ 723-DUCK Renovated World War II amphibious vehicles tour historic Boston and then splash into the Charles River. Tours (Apr–Nov) leave daily half-hourly, from Prudential Center, 101 Huntington Avenue.

WHALEWATCHING AND BOAT TOURS
Aquarium whalewatch trips (➤ 46)
Boston Harbor Cruises ✉ 1 Long Wharf ☎ 227-4321 Whalewatch trips, sightseeing cruises, sunset cruises, shuttle service to J.F.K. Library & Museum (➤ 48) 🕐 Daily
Bay State Cruises ✉ 67 Long Wharf ☎ 723-7800 Whalewatch trips, harbor cruises, Boston Harbor Islands, Cape Cod. 🕐 Daily Jun–Aug, weekends May, Sep–Oct
Massachusetts Bay Lines ✉ Rowes Wharf ☎ 542-8000 Harbor tours, lighthouse, entertainment cruises. 🕐 Year-round.

Out of Boston Tours
Gray Line ☎ 236-2148 operate tours to Cambridge/Lexington/ Concord, Plimoth Plantation and Plymouth Rock, Salem, Newport, Cape Cod. Pick up from major Boston and Cambridge hotels. Spring to fall.

Bostonian trolley bus

EXCURSIONS

An excursion out of Boston gives you the chance to see some New England countryside, not to mention all those picture-postcard clapboard houses. The places described below are easily accessible by public transportation. Train schedules are available at some T stations.

CONCORD

A lot of history is packed into Concord, a small, pretty town with pleasant shops and places to eat and stay. In Revolutionary Concord, the key point is the North Bridge (¾ mile from the center of town), where on April 19, 1775, the first battle in the Revolution took place. This is commemorated by Daniel Chester French's *Minute Man* statue. There's also Literary Concord: in the 19th century an influential group of writers and transcendentalist thinkers lived here including Nathaniel Hawthorne, Bronson and Louisa May Alcott, Ralph Waldo Emerson, and Henry Thoreau. Their houses are open to the public (some seasonally). All are buried in Sleepy Hollow Cemetery. The Concord Museum draws the threads together, with exhibits such as one of the two lanterns that were hung in the steeple of Old North Church as a signal to the patriots, and a re-creation of Emerson's study.

LOWELL

Anyone interested in industrial archaeology or textiles will glean a lot of information from Lowell, the town where the Industrial Revolution began in the U.S. A highly acclaimed urban regeneration scheme has restored many cotton mills and 5½ miles of canals. In summer, visitors tour this

INFORMATION

Concord
Distance About 20 miles
Journey time 40 minutes

🕐 Emerson's and Hawthorne's houses closed winter; other sites open all year, hours vary

🚆 Regular trains from North Station

➕ Off map to northwest

ℹ️ Greater Merrimack Valley Visitors Bureau

✉️ 22 Shattuck Street, Lowell, MA 01852

☎️ 508/459-6150

Lowell
Distance About 30 miles
Journey time 45 minutes

🕐 All open daily except Whistler House closed Jan–Feb; Visitor Center: 9-5. Other sites: hours vary

🚆 Hourly trains from North Station, then shuttle bus to downtown

➕ Off map to northwest

ℹ️ Market Mills Visitor Center

✉️ 246 Market Street, Lowell MA 01852

☎️ 508/954-8030

🅿️ Reservations needed for tours

Minute Man, *Concord*

National Historical Park area of the town by canalboat and trolley, in winter by ranger-led and self-guided walk. The Market Mills Visitor Center gives a good introduction and is the starting point for tours. In Boott Cotton Mills Museum the weave room has 88 looms in operation (free ear-plugs are supplied on request!) and the Working People Exhibit, in former mill-workers' housing, gives a good picture of the life led by the workers. Lowell is also the new home of the Sports Museum of New England (▶ 53), worth a visit if you're a fan.

SALEM

To most people Salem means first and foremost witches. The town certainly makes the most of it, with a range of interpretations of the mass hysteria of the 1690s. The best of the bunch is the Salem Witch Museum. However, the town also has a particularly rich maritime history and, resulting from it, some of the best Federal architecture in America. In the 18th and early 19th centuries Salem's prosperous ship builders, sea captains and merchants built graceful houses and filled them with beautiful things. Many of these objects are now in the Peabody Essex Museum, a vast collection of Far Eastern decorative arts, furniture, maritime painting, and Native and Early American artifacts.

PLYMOUTH

The landing of the Pilgrims in 1620 (the exact location is debated) is commemorated on the town's waterfront by Plymouth Rock. Docked next to it is the replica *Mayflower II*, which visitors can board. Three miles south is Plimoth Plantation, a meticulously accurate reproduction of the Pilgrims' settlement as it was in 1627. As on *Mayflower II*, "interpreters" in period costume faithfully act out the parts, chatting with visitors while getting on with daily chores. At the Wampanoag Indian Homesite, Native Americans, on whose ancestors' land the Pilgrims settled, tell of their experiences.

Peabody Museum, Salem

INFORMATION

Salem
Distance About 16 miles
Journey time 30 minutes
◉ Peabody Essex Museum closed Mon in winter. Witch Museum open daily
🚉 Hourly trains from North Station
ℹ Salem Office of Tourism
✉ 93 Washington Street, Salem MA 01970
☎ 508/745-9595; 800/777-6848

Plymouth
Distance About 50 miles
Journey time About 1 hour
◉ Plimoth Plantation, *Mayflower II*: Apr–Nov
✉ Plimoth Plantation
☎ 508/746-1622
ℹ Plymouth Visitor Information
✉ North Park Avenue, Plymouth, MA 02361
☎ 508/747-7525

WHAT'S ON

January	*Martin Luther King weekend*
February	*Chinese New Year* (Jan/Feb)
March	*Spring Flower Show* (mid-month) *St. Patrick's Day Parade*
April	*Boston Marathon* (third Mon) *Kite Festival* (second Sat): Franklin Park
May	*Harvard Square Book Festival* *Boston Pops Concerts*: season starts early May
June	*Battle of Bunker Hill re-enactment*: (Sunday before Bunker Hill Day, Jun 17) *Harborlights Music Festival* (Jun to Sep): Waterfront concerts *Boston Globe Jazz Festival*: Hatch Shell
July	*Boston Pops Concerts*: free outdoor concerts *Independence celebrations* (week of Jul 4): Boston Pops concert with fireworks, Boston Harborfest music festival, and U.S.S. *Constitution* turnaround *Italian* feste (*street festivals*) (Jul/Aug weekends): in North End
August	*Moon Festival*: processions in Chinatown
September	*Cambridge River Festival*: events on the river
October	*Columbus Day Parade* *Head of the Charles Regatta* (3rd week) *Boston Symphony Orchestra*: season Oct–Apr
November	*Christmas tree lighting ceremonies*: Faneuil Marketplace and Charles Square, Cambridge *Boston Ballet*: *The Nutcracker* (Nov–Dec): Wang Center
December	*Tree lighting ceremonies*: Prudential Center, Harvard Square *Boston Tea Party* (mid-Dec): re-enactment *Carol concert*: Trinity Church, Copley Square *New Year's Eve*: First Night celebrations

BOSTON's
top 25 sights

The sights are shown on the maps on the inside front cover and inside back cover, numbered **1–25** *from west to east across the city*

LONGFELLOW HOUSE & BRATTLE STREET

DID YOU KNOW?

- Longfellow could speak 8 languages and read and write in 12

INFORMATION

- ✚ B2
- ✉ 105 Brattle Street, Cambridge
- ☎ 876-4492
- 🕐 Wed–Fri 12–4:30; Sat, Sun 10–4:30. Call to confirm winter opening times
- 🍴 No
- 🚇 Harvard Square (then pleasant ½ mile walk)
- ♿ Garden good; house with staff assistance
- 💲 Cheap
- ↔ Harvard Square and University (➤ 25), Harvard University Museums (➤ 26)
- ❓ House tours

The clapboard houses on Brattle Street in Cambridge are particularly beautiful examples of colonial architecture. One of them, Longfellow House, was Washington's base in the Revolution and later the home of one of America's best-loved poets.

Tory Row Brattle Street begins close to Harvard Square. During the pre-Revolutionary 1770s the land on either side was owned by loyalist families, forced to quit when the patriots took over the area in 1774. No. 42, Brattle House, home of one such Tory, was later lived in by the feminist Margaret Fuller. The Dexter Pratt House, No. 56, now a bakery, was the home of the blacksmith of Longfellow's poem *The Village Blacksmith*. The shingle-fronted Stoughton House, No. 90, was designed by H. H. Richardson of Trinity Church fame (➤ 32).

Longfellow House No. 105, built in 1759 on an estate that extended down to the river, was George Washington's base during the siege of Boston, 1775–76. The widow of a later owner took in lodgers and thus, in 1837, came Henry Wadsworth Longfellow, the new Professor of Modern Languages at Harvard University. He later married Frances "Fanny" Appleton, whose wealthy mill-owning father bought the house for them. Happily married, they raised six children here, entertaining the intellectuals of the day. It was here that Longfellow wrote many of his poems, including the *Song of Hiawatha* and *Paul Revere's Ride*. Take the tour through the dining room, parlor, library, bedrooms and, of course, Longfellow's study.

Top: Longfellow House
Above: Henry Wadsworth Longfellow

2

HARVARD SQUARE & HARVARD UNIVERSITY

One of the most significant strands in the fabric of Bostonian life is the academic scene. In Cambridge you can walk through hallowed Harvard Yard in the footsteps of the great and famous, then see what today's students are up to in Harvard Square.

Harvard University Among the first things the Massachusetts Bay colonists did was to provide for the training of ministers, and thus was founded, in 1636, what became one of the world's most respected seats of learning. Most of its historic buildings are in Harvard Yard, entered across the street from the First Parish Church. Ahead, in front of Bulfinch's granite University Hall, is a statue by Daniel Chester French of benefactor John Harvard, famous for its "three lies" (Harvard was not the founder; a student, not Harvard, was the model; the foundation date is wrong). The elegant 18th-century redbrick halls grouped around this, the Old Yard, are dormitories. Behind University Hall is New Yard, with Memorial Church on the left facing the pillared façade of Widener Library. Groups of students move quietly across the grassy lawns. Pass beside H. H. Richardson's Sever Hall to emerge in Quincy Street opposite the Carpenter Center for the Visual Arts, the only Le Corbusier building in North America. The Fogg Art Museum (➤ 26) is next door. Radcliffe College, formerly a women's college, is alongside Cambridge Common, centered on the lovely Radcliffe Yard.

Harvard Square The newsstand by the T is a famous landmark in this irregularly shaped "square." In and around it you can watch chess games, listen to street musicians, sit in a sidewalk café, shop for trendy clothes, or go to a club for jazz, blues, or reggae.

Strolling through Harvard Square

HIGHLIGHTS

- Harvard Yard
- Radcliffe Yard

INFORMATION

✚ C2

✉ Harvard University: Harvard Yard, Peabody Street, Cambridge

☎ Harvard Square Visitor Information Booth: 1-800/862-5678; University 495-1573

🕐 Daily

🍴 Plenty in Harvard Square area

🚇 Harvard

♿ Free

↔ Longfellow House (➤ 24), Harvard University Museums (➤ 26)

❓ Campus tours Mon–Fri 10, 2; Sat 2

25

HARVARD UNIVERSITY MUSEUMS

HIGHLIGHTS

- Italian Early Renaissance paintings (Fogg)
- Impressionists (Fogg)
- Jade (Sackler)
- Glass flowers (Botanical)

INFORMATION

- ✛ C2
- ✉ Fogg & Busch-Reisinger: 32 Quincy Street. Sackler: 485 Broadway, Cambridge
- ☎ 495-9400 (both)
  Botanical: 26 Oxford Street; Peabody: 11 Divinity Avenue
- ☎ 495-3045
- ◷ Mon–Sat 9–5 (Art Museums 10–5); Sun 1–5
- ♿ Very good
- Ⓜ Moderate; free Sat AM

Top: Fogg Art Museum
Below: The Crucifixion by Lorenzetti Ambrogio

Few universities have such an enviable collection. The pieces in Harvard's three art museums, each of which has its own character, are of a quality to rival any in the world. This is where to spend Saturday morning—it's free then.

The art museums The galleries of the Fogg Art Museum are arranged around a Renaissance-style arcaded courtyard, a delightful setting for a remarkable collection of Western art. The Italian Early Renaissance period is particularly well represented, with gems from artists such as Simone Martini, Bernardo Daddi and Filippo Lippi. Other rooms cover Dutch and Flemish painting. Upstairs galleries feature major American landscape painters and an outstanding collection with familiar pieces by all the major Impressionists and some important Picassos.

The small Busch-Reisinger Museum, reached through the upper floor of the Fogg, focuses on Expressionist art of Central and Northern Europe, with Bauhaus artifacts and paintings by Kandinsky, Klee, and Moholy-Nagy.

The Arthur M. Sackler Museum next door to the Fogg, at the corner of Quincy Street and Broadway, is in a building by Sir James Stirling. Along with one of the best collections of Chinese jade in the world, it has Chinese bronzes, Japanese prints, and Greek and Roman vases and sculptures—all superb examples.

Museums of Cultural & Natural History This is a large complex of four adjoining museums. For most visitors the highlight is the Botanical Museum's Glass Flowers exhibit, 3,000 glass models of 830 species of flower. The Peabody Museum is devoted to anthropology.

ISABELLA STEWART GARDNER MUSEUM

This is the sort of treat you either indulge yourself in at once or you save for last, depending on your nature. It is one woman's personal collection of treasures displayed in the Venetian-style house she built around an exquisite courtyard.

"Beautiful things" Determined to give her "very young country" the opportunity of "seeing beautiful things," the much-traveled (and independently wealthy) Mrs. Gardner made a start in 1896 by buying a Rembrandt self-portrait. Her collection grew to include work by artists such as Giotto, Botticelli, Raphael, Vermeer, Degas, and Matisse, as well as her friends John Singer Sargent and James McNeill Whistler. She also acquired prints and drawings, books, sculptures, ceramics and glass, carpets, tapestries, lace, stained glass, and furniture.

Music and horticulture The building itself, known as Fenway Court, and the atmosphere that pervades it, is as much the creation of Mrs. Gardner as her collection. She arranged her objects in a series of rooms—the Raphael Room, the Titian Room, the Gothic Room, and more. She filled the courtyard with sculptures, plants and trees, and she celebrated the opening of her home (she lived on the top floor) to the public with a concert given by members of the Boston Symphony Orchestra. Today, concerts are held in the Tapestry Room on winter weekends.

Art heist The collection suffered a terrible loss—and America's biggest art theft—in March 1990 when thieves dressed as policemen made off with 13 items. Among them were a priceless Vermeer and *The Sea of Galilee*, Rembrandt's only seascape. The pieces are still missing, and empty frames are a poignant reminder.

HIGHLIGHTS

- The courtyard, at any season
- *El Jaleo*, JS Sargent
- *Presentation of the Infant Jesus in the Temple*, Giotto
- Afternoon concerts on winter weekends

INFORMATION

- ✚ D6
- ✉ 280 Fenway, Back Bay
- ☎ 566-1401
- 🕐 Tue–Sun 11–5. Closed most Mon
- 🍽 On premises
- Ⓜ Museum (green line E)
- ♿ Good
- 💲 Expensive
- ↔ Museum of Fine Arts (➤ 28)
- ❓ Concerts Sep–Apr: Sat, Sun 1:30 ☎ 734-1359. Tours weekly. Lectures. Shop

The courtyard—fountains, ferns and fragrant flowering plants

5

MUSEUM OF FINE ARTS

HIGHLIGHTS

- Nubian collection
- Impressionist room
- Copley portraits
- Tang dynasty earthenware

INFORMATION

- ✚ E6
- ✉ 465 Huntington Avenue, Back Bay
- ☎ 267-9300
- ◷ Tue, Thu–Sat 10–4:45; Wed 10–9:45; Sun 10–5:45. West Wing Thu, Fri 5–9:45. Closed Mon
- 🍽 Choice on premises
- 🚇 Museum (green line E)
- ♿ Excellent
- 💵 Expensive; Wed 4–9:45 voluntary contribution
- ↔ Gardner Museum (▶ 27)
- ❓ Free guided walks, Tue–Sat Tea and Music Tue–Fri 2:30–4. Lectures, films, concerts. Good shop

Winslow Homer, Long Branch, *detail*

The MFA is one of America's foremost museums. The Asian collection is unrivaled in this hemisphere, the European art is superb, the American rooms excellent. You cannot possibly take it all in at once.

Asian, Egyptian, Classical The MFA's Nubian collection is the best outside the Sudan. It is all exquisite, from the neat rows of little shawabtis to the faience jewelry. The Egyptian rooms are popular, with amazing hieroglyphics and splendid statuary. In the Greek and Roman rooms, pick out the Attic red figure pottery. Buddhist sculptures, Chinese ceramics and Indian paintings make up part of an Asian collection outstanding in scope and quality. Outside, take in the Tenshin Garden.

European In the Evans Wing upstairs, seek out the little gem of a Rembrandt in a glass case, then take in works of Tiepolo, Gainsborough, Turner, Delacroix, Constable, and a goodly number of Millets. The Impressionist room is an array of familiar paintings, from Monet and Renoir to Mary Cassatt. There is porcelain from all over Europe and period rooms from Britain.

American New England furniture and decorative arts feature in a series of period rooms. Near the silver (note Paul Revere's work) is a fine musical instruments collection. As for the art of New England, downstairs in the Evans Wing, begin with the Copley portraits, work through the 19th-century landscape painters Bierstadt, Fitz Hugh Lane and Thomas Cole, and move on to Winslow Homer and John Singer Sargent, and, from the 20th century, Childe Hassam, Edward Hopper and Lilian Westacott Hale. In the Contemporary Art room find work by Georgia O'Keeffe and Stuart Davis.

CHRISTIAN SCIENCE CENTER

It is the scale of the Center that is so mind-blowing. The World Headquarters for the Church of Christ, Scientist, occupies 14 acres of prime Back Bay land, with a church seating 3,000. The main attraction, however, is the Mapparium.

World headquarters Perhaps the best place from which to appreciate the vast size of this complex is from the top of the Prudential Tower (▶ 30). From here you look straight down on its 270-ft. reflecting pool with, alongside it, the small granite original Mother Church and the huge domed basilica-type extension. At the far end of the pool is the Publishing Society building, while nearer the Pru are the office tower, the Sunday School building, and the Broadcasting Center.

The churches The Mother Church of Christian Science was founded in Boston in 1892 by Mary Baker Eddy. The original church building was opened in 1894 but the numbers of believers in spiritual healing grew so rapidly that an extension was built in 1906, seating 3,000. The huge open space here is dominated by one of the world's largest organs, played at every service.

Publishing and the Mapparium The *Christian Science Monitor* is a highly respected international daily newspaper, founded in 1908 by Mary Baker Eddy and read by many outside the movement for its unbiased reporting. The Publishing Society building also houses the highlight of the whole Center, the Mapparium, a huge brightly colored stained-glass globe. Walk into the center of the world and examine the political boundaries of the early 1930s, when the thing was made. Try out the echo—sound waves bounce back off the glass, creating decidedly weird effects.

Top: Mapparium
Above: the Mother Church

DID YOU KNOW?

- The Mapparium has 608 panels, each covering 10 degrees of latitude and longitude
- The Aeolian-Skinner church organ has 13,595 pipes

INFORMATION

- ✚ F6
- ✉ 175 Huntington Avenue
- ☎ 450-2000
- 🕐 Mapparium: Mon–Sat 10–4. Mother Church: Mon–Sat 10–4, Sun 11:15–2
- 🍴 Near by, in Prudential Center
- Ⓟ Prudential
- ♿ Good
- Free
- ↔ Prudential Tower Skywalk (▶ 30)
- ❓ Tours of the Mother Church daily

PRUDENTIAL & HANCOCK TOWERS

HIGHLIGHTS

- Reflection of Trinity Church
- Walter Muir Whitehill's voice-over (Hancock)
- Model of Boston in 1775 (Hancock)

INFORMATION

John Hancock Observatory

- ✚ F5
- ✉ Copley Square
- ☎ 572-6429
- ◉ All year Mon–Sat 9AM–11PM; Sun 10AM–11PM
- ⌷ Near by
- Ⓒ Copley
- ⚫ Excellent
- ⚫ Cheap
- ↔ Boston Public Library (➤ 31), Trinity Church (➤ 32)

Prudential Skywalk

- ✚ F6
- ✉ Prudential Tower, 800 Boylston Street
- ☎ 859-0648
- ◉ Daily 10–10
- ⌷ Top of the Hub (\$\$)
- Ⓒ Prudential
- ⚫ Excellent
- ⚫ Cheap
- ↔ Christian Science Center (➤ 29)

The Hancock Tower seen from the Pru

The question is not whether you should take a look at Boston from the top of a skyscraper, but which of these two you should go for—if you don't have time for both, that is. Try to do one in the daytime and the other after dark.

John Hancock Tower & Observatory There is something immensely serene about this icy shaft of blue glass thrusting upwards to join the clouds, no matter how ephemeral it looks beside Trinity Church, whose solid granite is reflected in its lowest windows. Designed by Ieoh Ming Pei in 1976 for the Prudential Insurance Company, the building caused a mighty sensation at first, particularly when its panes of glass kept popping out and smashing on the sidewalk below. But it has long since found a place in (most) Bostonians' hearts. An express elevator whisks you to the Observatory on the 60th floor; windows on three sides give all-round views. A lovely voice-over account by the architectural historian Walter Muir Whitehill of the city's changing topography guides you round the vista. A sound-and-light show features the events of 1775, and you can tune in to Logan air traffic controllers' radios.

Skywalk at the Prudential Tower Architecturally undistinguished, the Prudential Tower is part of the 1960s Prudential Center office and shopping complex. Take the wind-whistling elevator to the Skywalk View and Exhibit on the 50th floor for 360-degree views as far as (weather permitting) the hills of Vermont. A variety of interactive exhibits fill you in on some of Boston's great historical and sports events, as well as its most distinguished buildings and residents. On the 52nd floor is the Top of the Hub bar and restaurant.

BOSTON PUBLIC LIBRARY

This is no ordinary public library. Behind its august granite façade lies an opulent institution built in the style of a Renaissance palazzo and decorated with sculptures, murals, and paintings by some of the greatest artists of their day.

The education of the people A people's palace dedicated to the advancement of learning was what Charles Follen McKim was commissioned to design. An architectural landmark in the classical style, facing Richardson's Romanesque Trinity Church across Copley Square, it opened its doors to the public in 1895. It is now the Research Library, the General Library being housed in the adjoining 1972 Johnson Building.

Further treasures Pass between Bela Pratt's voluptuous bronzes, *Science* and *Art*, to enter through Daniel Chester French's bronze doors. Pause in the lobby to admire the zodiac patterning of the marble floor and the mosaic ceiling. Ascend the marble staircase, guarded by lions by Louis Saint-Gaudens (Augustus's brother), and from its windows catch a glimpse of the courtyard around which the library is built. The stairs and landing are decorated with panels by Puvis de Chavannes, whimsical representations of the muses of inspiration. One room on this floor has paintings depicting the quest for the Holy Grail, by Edwin Austin Abbey. On the next floor, awaiting restoration, are the John Singer Sargent murals, *Judaism* and *Christianity*, completed in 1916. Back downstairs, pass the silent reading rooms to find the colonnaded courtyard. Purple-leaved maples shade a pool bordered by dark green foliage. Sit for a while and enjoy the tranquility.

HIGHLIGHTS

- The courtyard
- Puvis de Chavannes murals
- John Singer Sargent murals
- Daniel Chester French bronze doors

INFORMATION

- ✚ F5
- ✉ Copley Square
- ☎ 536-5400
- ⏰ All year Mon–Thu 9–9; Fri–Sat 2–6. Oct–May, Sun 2–6. Closed Jun–Sep, Sun
- 🍴 Near by
- Ⓒ Copley
- ♿ Good
- 🎟 Free
- ⇄ John Hancock Tower (► 30), Trinity Church (► 32)
- ❓ Art and architecture tours Mon 2:30; Tue, Thu 6; Fri, Sat 11; Oct–May, Sun 2. Lectures

Top: staircase
Below: courtyard

TRINITY CHURCH

H. H. Richardson's prototype French Romanesque church is often described as America's masterpiece of ecclesiastical architecture. Sit beneath its mighty tower: a greater contrast to the fragility of John Hancock Tower next door can hardly be imagined.

Top: La Farge murals
Above: west front

HIGHLIGHTS

- Polychrome interior
- John La Farge paintings and lancet windows
- Decorated organ pipes
- Reflection in John Hancock Tower

INFORMATION

- F5
- Copley Square
- 536-0944
- Daily 8–6
- Near by
- Copley
- Good
- Free
- John Hancock Tower (► 30), Boston Public Library (► 31)
- Free half-hour organ recitals Fri 12:15

The plan The Back Bay was a newly developed landfill area when the Copley Square site was bought and Henry Hobson Richardson was commissioned, in 1872, to draw up designs for a new Trinity Church. Richardson based his layout on 11th-century Romanesque churches in the Auvergne, in France. A massive lantern tower over the transept crossing would dominate the church inside and out, requiring over 2,000 wooden piles massed together to support its granite foundations. Externally, the chunky granite blocks are broken up by bands of pink sandstone.

The interior Inside, John La Farge created an intricate polychrome interior, a tapestry of rich reds and greens highlighted with gold. The arches beneath the great tower are decorated with La Farge murals painted in 1876–77, and it was he who supervised the stained glass, some by Edward Burne-Jones and William Morris. La Farge's own small but vibrant, turquoise lancet windows are in the north transept, west wall. The decorated pipes of the organ in the west end are notable (music at Trinity is important). In the Baptistry is a bust by Daniel Chester French of the portly rector Phillips Brooks, whose greatest claim to fame is his carol "O Little Town of Bethlehem." His full-length statue, by Augustus Saint-Gaudens, stands outside the north transept. At the east end there is a small cloister and garden.

BACK BAY & COMMONWEALTH AVENUE

A Parisian-style boulevard lined with the grandest houses in Boston is the centerpiece of an amazing piece of 19th-century urban planning. To walk down it is to be transported to a different age.

Landfill By the 1850s, Boston, still a small peninsula, was getting overcrowded. Desperate for building land, developers turned to the swampy "back bay" of the Charles River, embarking on a remarkable landfill project to create a whole new residential district. Inspired by Paris's boulevard system, the architect Arthur Gilman planned a grid, eight blocks long and four blocks wide, with a long central mall. Block by block, the new houses went up and the wealthy moved in.

Commonwealth Avenue The *nouveau-riche* industrialists who flocked to the Back Bay felt none of the Puritan restraints of the Proper Bostonians of Beacon Hill, and their rows of ostentatious brownstones are an exuberant blend of Victorian architectural styles. The centerpiece is Commonwealth Avenue. Central gardens are lined with trees; in spring magnolias bloom in profusion. A string of statues includes slavery abolitionist William Lloyd Garrison and naval historian Samuel Eliot Morison. Find your own favorite houses—almost every one has something worthy of note. Most are now apartments, some are offices. The château-like Burrage Mansion at Hereford Street stands out, with statuettes all over the place. To see inside a more average home, visit Gibson House on Beacon Street (► 52). After strolling down Commonwealth Avenue, walk back along Newbury Street for some stylish window shopping (► 70). Also check out the Newbury Street *trompe l'oeil* murals at the Boston Architectural Center and number 354.

Samuel Eliot Morison statue, Commonwealth Avenue

HIGHLIGHTS

- Houses on Commonwealth Avenue
- People-watching in the Newbury Street cafés
- Window-shopping in Newbury Street

DID YOU KNOW?

- North–south streets are named alphabetically, Arlington to Hereford

INFORMATION

- F–G 5
- Newbury and Boylston streets
- Arlington, Copley, Hynes
- Christian Science Center (► 29), Hancock Tower (► 30), Prudential Tower (► 30), Boston Public Library (► 31), Trinity Church (► 32), Public Garden (► 36)

MUSEUM OF SCIENCE

HIGHLIGHTS

- The T-Rex
- Making a skeleton work an exercise bike
- Smelling a skunk
- Mugar Omni Theater shows

INFORMATION

- G3
- Science Park
- 723-2500
- July 5–Labor Day daily 9–7, Fri 9–9. Labor Day–Jul 4 daily 9–5, Fri 9–9. Extended hours over school vacations
- Three on premises
- Science Park
- Excellent; sight and hearing impaired facilities
- Expensive; separate tickets for Planetarium, Laser Show, Omni Theater; combination ticket discounts
- Good shop

This whole place buzzes and hums. Excited children run from one exhibit to another, pressing buttons and peering into the 450 entertaining, interactive exhibits. There's always plenty to do.

Science now The museum prides itself on being at the cutting edge of science education. It's in a fine position, straddling the Charles River.

"It's awesome" At the far end of the Blue Wing, check on the times of the indoor lightning demos. On the same floor, have fun with a wave tank or play with mathematical models. A 20-ft. T. Rex peers at you over the rails from the lower level, where you can test your memory and hand/eye coordination. In the Green Wing, on the lower level, the Human Body is a popular exhibit, with its exercising skeleton. If you so wish, you can inflate a (real) sheep's lungs. Up a floor you can smell skunk at Squam Lake, and up again, on level two, you can check your powers of observation in Seeing the Unseen. Then test your engineering skills in Investigate!, on level two in the Blue Wing.

Mugar Omni, Planetarium, and Lasers Lie back and be totally enveloped in the sight and sound of an IMAX film in the five-story domed screen of the Mugar Omni Theater with its 84-speaker sound system. Multi-media presentations at the Planetarium cover various astronomical subjects and, for older children and adults, there are evening laser programs.

BEACON HILL & LOUISBURG SQUARE

Beacon Hill is an enclave of elegant redbrick houses in a leafy maze of steep streets and narrow cobbled lanes. It has been the bastion of the Boston Brahmin since the early 1800s.

Brahmin stronghold After the opening of the new State House on its southern slope, Beacon Hill was developed as a prestigious residential district by a group of entrepreneurs that included architect Charles Bulfinch (► 12). Boston's top families swiftly moved in. Rich as they were, these Brahmins were also the personification of Puritan reserve. Showiness was taboo, so their new houses were the epitome of restraint, elegant doorways and delicate ironwork gracing plain brick façades.

Perfectly preserved To get the magic of it all, choose a sunny day and just wander, noting the pillared porticoes, genteel fanlights and flowery windowboxes. The Beacon Hill walk (► 16) leads you to some of the most treasured corners, including Mt. Vernon Street, Chestnut Street, tiny Acorn Street and, best of all, Louisburg Square. Here Bulfinch's lovely bowfronts look onto a central garden reminiscent of a European square. Notice how the street lamps are lit all day and, in Beacon Street, look for the purple panes: manganese oxide in a batch of glass reacted with sunlight to produce discolored but, now, highly prized and very distinctive panes. To see inside a Beacon Hill home, visit the Nichols House (► 53). On the hill's north slope from Pinckney Street down to Cambridge Street, the houses are smaller and more varied in style, the overall effect less grand. It has several important sites in the history of Boston's African-American community (► 53).

HIGHLIGHTS

* Louisburg Square
* Pinckney Street and its view of Charles River
* Purple panes of glass, Beacon Street
* Charles Street shops and restaurants

INFORMATION

* a–b III–IV/G4
* Bounded by Beacon Street, Embankment Road, Cambridge Street, Bowdoin Street
* Choice in Charles Street
* Park, Charles, Arlington, Bowdoin (closed Sat)
* Steep hills, some uneven surfaces
* Boston Common & Public Garden (► 36), Harrison Gray Otis House (► 37), State House (► 38), Boston Athenaeum (► 39)
* SPNEA tours of Beacon Hill (► 37), Black Heritage Trail: see Museum of Afro-American History (► 53)

BOSTON COMMON & THE PUBLIC GARDEN

Top: Swan Boats, Public Garden
Above: Boston Common

DID YOU KNOW?

- The Swan Boats were inspired by Wagner's *Lohengrin*

INFORMATION

- a–b IV/G5
- Bounded by Beacon Street, Park Street, Tremont Street, Boylston Street, Arlington Street
- Swan Boats: 522-1966. Boston Common Visitor Center: 522-2639
- Public Garden: daily dawn–10PM. Swan Boats Apr–Sep
- Near by
- Park, Boylston, Arlington
- Good
- Garden and Common free. Swan Boats cheap
- Beacon Hill (▶ 35), Harrison Gray Otis House (▶ 37), State House (▶ 38), Boston Athenaeum (▶ 39)

Very different in history and in character, these adjoining pieces of public open space, separated by Charles Street right in the heart of the city, are held in deep affection. Without them, Boston just wouldn't be Boston.

Boston Common The oldest public park in the United States owes its origins to early English settlers who in 1634 acquired the land from a Reverend William Blaxton, for common grazing. Being common land, it was also where criminals were hanged, witches were dunked and the dead were buried (in the Central Burying Ground, by Boylston Street). Here, British soldiers camped and George Washington addressed the crowds after Independence. Early in the 1800s the gallows were removed, cattle were banned, paths were laid out, fountains and monuments erected. It is still a place for speeches and demos, but also for sports, for paddling or skating in Frog Pond, chasing the pigeons, eating ice cream, listening to street performers and concerts—and people-watching. Perfectly safe by day, it's best avoided at night.

The Public Garden Much more genteel and decorative, this was created as a botanical garden, in 1837, from reclaimed marshland. Hundreds of beautiful trees were planted, and beds, lawns and a lacing of footpaths were laid out. The garden is perennially beautiful and often fairytale-like. The centerpiece is a pond, with a little cast-iron suspension bridge. Here, in summer, you can ride the famous Swan Boats and, in winter, you can skate. Sculptures include an equestrian *George Washington* (Thomas Ball, 1869), Bela Pratt's *Edward Everett Hale* (1913), the Ether Monument, marking its first use as an anesthetic in 1846, and *Make Way for Ducklings* (▶ 59).

HARRISON GRAY OTIS HOUSE

This is Boston's only remaining example of a Federal-style mansion. Meticulously restored in its every detail, the gracious interior is a very accurate representation of how the upper classes lived in the 19th century.

Otis and Bulfinch One of the leading lights in post-Revolutionary Boston politics was the lawyer Harrison Gray Otis (1765–1844), long-standing friend of architect Charles Bulfinch. A wealthy man moving in the upper echelons of Bostonian society, in 1796 he commissioned Bulfinch to build him this grand mansion in what was then the elegant area of Bowdoin Square. The structure's very restrained, very proper, brick façade is typical of what became known as the Federal style. Five years later, Bulfinch built Otis an even bigger house on newly developed Beacon Hill (➤ 35), to which all the wealthy were rapidly migrating. By the 1830s the Otis home had become a boarding house. Now the Otis House and the Old West Church next door are a little oasis of elegance in an area of less-than-lovely urban renewal.

The SPNEA In 1916 the Society for the Preservation of New England Antiquities bought the property as its headquarters. Accuracy and authenticity being its hallmarks, the SPNEA has restored the interior with reproduction wallpapers and paint colors based on paint analysis (there are some surprisingly bright yellows and turquoises). Otis and his wife, Sally, were lavish entertainers and the parlor, dining room and second-floor drawing room, all brightly colored and furnished in high Federal style, provide an insight into social manners of the day, while bedrooms, kitchens and servant quarters give you a glimpse of family life.

HIGHLIGHTS

- Bulfinch Federal design
- Reproductions of original wallpaper
- Colors of original paintwork
- Federal era furniture

DID YOU KNOW?

- In 1926 the house was moved back 40ft because of road widening

INFORMATION

- ✚ bIII/G4
- ✉ 141 Cambridge Street
- ☎ 227-3956
- 🕐 Tue–Fri 12–5; Sat 10–5
- 🍴 None
- 🚇 Bowdoin (closed Sat), Charles, Government Center
- ♿ Wheelchairs first floor only
- 💲 Moderate; SPNEA members free
- ↔ Beacon Hill (➤ 35), State House (➤ 38), Boston Athenaeum (➤ 39)
- ❓ House tours on the hour (last at 4). Walking tours of Beacon Hill mid-May–mid-Oct, Sat (call ahead). Shop

MASSACHUSETTS STATE HOUSE

HIGHLIGHTS

- Gold dome
- Sacred Cod
- Senate Reception Room
- Senate Chamber

DID YOU KNOW?

- When the Sacred Cod was stolen by students in 1933, no sessions could be held for three days
- If Republicans gain power, the Sacred Cod will be turned to face the other way
- From 1825 to 1928 the brick façade was painted
- Road distances out of Boston are measured from the dome

INFORMATION

- ✚ bIII–IV/G4
- ✉ Beacon Street
- ☎ 727-3676
- 🕐 Mon–Fri 10–4
- 🍴 None
- 🎐 Park
- ♿ Partial wheelchair access
- 🎟 Free
- ↔ Beacon Hill (➤ 35), Harrison Gray Otis House (➤ 37), Boston Athenaeum (➤ 39)
- 🅿 Tours (45 minutes) every ½ hour

Prosperous and newly independent in the late 18th century, Massachusetts needed a larger, more imposing State House. Charles Bulfinch's masterpiece is a landmark in American architecture.

Hub of the Hub Bulfinch began designing the new state house on his return from England, much influenced by Robert Adam's Renaissance style. Construction began in 1795 on a prominent piece of Beacon Hill land presented by the wealthy merchant and patriot John Hancock. Cut off in your mind's eye the side wings (an early 20th-century addition), and focus on Bulfinch's dignified two-story portico and the glistening dome. Its original shingles were covered in copper from the foundry of Paul Revere when the roof began to leak, and the gold leaf was added in 1874.

Seat of government At the top of the steps, go through a side door into the columned Doric Hall (the central door is for visiting presidents and retiring governors only). From here pass through the marble Nurses' Hall and note the Chester French statue of Civil War hero William Bartlett and Bela Pratt's memorial to Civil War nurses. The Italian marble floor in the Hall of Flags was laid by immigrants from Italy living in the North End. Up the staircase, in the 1895 extension, is the House of Representatives chamber. Here, the Sacred Cod, a symbol of the importance of the fishing industry and a lucky mascot, must hang whenever the 160 state representatives are in session. The dignified barrel-vaulted and Ionic-columned Senate Reception Room is Bulfinch's, as is the Senate Chamber, where 40 senators debate beneath a graceful sunburst dome. A larger-than-life *JFK* (Isabel McIlvain, 1988) is one of several statues outside.

BOSTON ATHENAEUM

Though many Bostonians have never been here, you must see what they are missing. Leave 20th-century hassle and noise behind and enter what Henry James called the "haunt of all the most civilised".

Temple of culture When the Athenaeum library moved here in 1849 it had been the center of both intellectual and cultural life in Boston for over 40 years. Indeed, the paintings and sculptures it had accumulated were to form the core of the Museum of Fine Arts' founding collection. An independent library, it remains the haunt of Boston's intellectual élite.

Escape Begin with the newspaper and periodical reading room. Oriental rugs cover the floors, the walls are lined with books, and leather-upholstered chairs are drawn up to a long table lit by table lamps and spread with historical and philological journals. The only sound is the ticking of the clock. Across the hall is a table covered with new books and an armchair set by the long window overlooking the Old Granary Burying Ground. Take the splendid old elevator to the blue-and-cream Bow Room and Long Room on the next floor, where art and antiques journals and the latest art books are set out. Only female members may sit and read on the sofa of the Ladies' Room. Also on this floor is the Print Room's outstanding collection. There are fresh flowers in every room, busts and statues stand in niches, and paintings hang in any space not taken up with books. Other floors can be viewed by pre-arranged tour and hold treasures such as the King's Chapel library, sent to the colony by William and Mary in 1698, and Washington's personal library. The reading room on the top floor is the ultimate haven, with individual desks by the full-length windows.

HIGHLIGHTS

- Main reading room, top floor
- Long Room and Bow Room
- Portraits, sculptures, rugs
- Views of Old Granary Burying Ground

DID YOU KNOW?

- Afternoon tea is served to members on Wednesdays
- The fresh flowers are funded by a gift honoring a former member

INFORMATION

- ✚ c1V/G4
- ✉ 10 1/2 Beacon Street
- ☎ 227-0270
- 🕐 First and second floors: Mon 9–8; Tue–Fri 9–5.30. Also Sep–May, Sat 9–4. Other floors: by tour only Tue, Thu at 3 (book ahead)
- 🍴 Near by
- 🅿 Park
- ♿ Wheelchair access
- 🆓 Free
- ↔ Beacon Hill (▶ 35), Harrison Gray Otis House (▶ 37), Massachusetts State House (▶ 38),
- ❓ Tours Tue, Thu at 3 (book ahead; free). Lectures. Concerts

17

OLD SOUTH MEETING HOUSE

HIGHLIGHTS

- Plain Puritan interior
- Box pews
- Tea Party audios

INFORMATION

✚ clV/H5
✉ Washington Street at Milk Street
☎ 482-6439
⏰ Tours Thu 12:15
🍴 On premises
Ⓜ State, Downtown Crossing
♿ Good
✋ Moderate
↔ Old State House (► 41)
❓ Concerts, lectures. Shop

Portrait of early settler etched onto glass

What started life in 1730 as a traditional Puritan meeting house was later, by reason only of its size, to witness one of the most significant moments in American and British history.

Sanctuary of freedom When things started to heat up in the years leading up to the Revolution, the town hall, Faneuil Hall, could no longer hold the crowds that were turning up, so this, the most spacious meeting place in the city, became their venue. Here the sparks of insurrection fanned by such speakers as Samuel Adams, James Otis, and John Hancock ignited on the evening of December 16, 1773. For it was here that night that Adams famously declared "Gentlemen, this meeting can do nothing more to save the country"—the signal for a band of men disguised as Mohawk Indians to lead the people off to the harbor and the so-called Boston Tea Party (► 12).

In the siege of Boston that followed, British troops occupied Old South, ripping out the pews and using it as a riding school for the cavalry. After the Revolution, it was restored as a church, but in 1872 was replaced by the New Old South Church, located on the corner of Copley Square. Threatened with demolition, Old South was saved for its historical associations and has been a museum ever since. The plain white-painted pews and pulpit of this simple brick church are reproductions, but the two-tiered gallery is original. The many exhibits, including a model of colonial Boston and audios of fiery debates, tell the whole Tea Party story in graphic detail.

OLD STATE HOUSE

This is the city's oldest public building, once the seat of British colonial government. It seems so tiny now, surrounded as it is by taller—but far less significant—buildings.

Colonial capitol Built in 1713 to replace an earlier Town House, the Old State House was the British governor's seat of office, home to the judicial court and to the Massachusetts Assembly. As such it was the scene of many a confrontation between the colonists and their rulers. It was here that James Otis railed against the "tyranny of taxation without representation" and it was under the balcony at the east end that the "Boston Massacre" took place in 1770: five colonists were killed in a clash with British soldiers, a key event preceding the Revolution. From the same balcony, the Declaration of Independence was read on July 18, 1776. At this point the gilded lion and unicorn on the east front, symbols of the British crown, were destroyed. From 1780 until Bulfinch's new State House was opened on Beacon Hill in 1798, this was the Massachusetts State House. For most of the 19th century it was used for commercial purposes, gradually falling into disrepair until the Boston Society was founded in 1881 to restore the building. The lion and unicorn were returned to their place, balanced now by the American eagle and the Massachusetts seal on the west end.

A museum of Boston The building is now home to the Bostonian Society's excellent museum. It traces the city's topographical, political, economic and social history with a fine collection of maritime art and artifacts, revolutionary memorabilia, prints, domestic objects, and audio exhibits.

HIGHLIGHTS

- Lion and unicorn
- Balcony from which Declaration of Independence was read

INFORMATION

- clll/H4
- 206 Washington Street
- 720-3290
- Daily 9:30–5
- Near by
- State
- Good
- Cheap
- Old South Meeting House (▶ 40), Faneuil Hall (▶ 42)
- Shop

19

FANEUIL HALL & MARKETPLACE

Faneuil Hall

Faneuil Hall is a landmark for all Americans, the place where the iniquities of the British government were first debated in the 1770s. Nowadays its marketplace is a landmark for visitors of every nation—as well as for Bostonians.

The Cradle of Liberty A wealthy trader of Huguenot origins, Peter Faneuil (pronounced "Fannel" or to rhyme with Dan-iel), presented the town with a market hall with a meeting room above. Ever since, the lower hall has been a market, and the galleried upper hall has been a place for public gatherings. In the 1700s, because the town meetings frequently discussed problems with Britain, Faneuil Hall became known as America's Cradle of Liberty. Since then national issues from the abolition of slavery to the Vietnam War have been aired here. If it is not in use, it's worth going in to hear the guide's account of the Revolution. The room bears all the hallmarks of Bulfinch, who expanded it in 1805. On the roof, look for the grasshopper weathervane.

Quincy's marketplace The Bulfinch expansion soon proved to be inadequate as more space was needed. In 1826, with an inspired piece of town planning that radically changed Boston's water-front, mayor Josiah Quincy filled in Town Dock and built over the wharves, providing a granite market hall flanked by granite warehouses. These were a wholesale food market until the 1960s. In the 1970s the area was renovated and revitalized, and is now the city's main tourist attraction (known as either Faneuil Hall Marketplace or Quincy Market) with dozens of shops, push-carts, stands, eating places and street entertainers. The Durgin Park Dining Rooms are an institution (▶ 62).

HIGHLIGHTS

- Bulfinch meeting room
- Grasshopper weathervane
- Quincy's granite market buildings
- Street entertainers

INFORMATION

- ✚ dlll/H4
- ✉ Congress Street
- ☎ 242-5642
- ◷ Faneuil Hall meeting room: 9–5 when not in use
- 🍴 A plethora
- 🚇 State, Aquarium, Government Center
- ♿ Good
- Meeting room free
- ↔ Old State House (▶ 41)
- ❓ Meeting room: 15-minute talk every ½ hour

U.S.S. *CONSTITUTION* & CHARLESTOWN

"Old Ironsides," as she is widely known by schoolchildren, is the oldest commissioned warship afloat in the world. She is moored in the Charlestown Navy Yard, a short, pleasant boat ride away across the Charles River.

The Navy Yard From 1800 to 1974 the Charles River navy yard played an important role building, repairing and supplying Navy warships. Its mission now is to interpret the history of naval shipbuilding. Representing the ships built here are U.S.S. *Constitution* and the World War II destroyer U.S.S. *Cassin Young*, both of which may be boarded. The old granite Building 22 now houses the U.S.S. *Constitution* Museum, where journals, artifacts and other exhibits record the frigate's 200-year career in both war and peace and give a picture of life aboard. Also open is the Commandant's House. The Bunker Hill Pavilion's multimedia show, "Whites of Their Eyes," tells the story of the Battle of Bunker Hill, which actually took place near by on Breed's Hill, on which stands the Bunker Hill Monument (► 55). The Monument is visible from and within walking distance of the yard.

U.S.S. *Constitution* The highlight of the Navy Yard is "Old Ironsides." Launched in Boston in 1797, she is still part of the U.S. Navy, whose sailors show visitors round the cramped quarters and stand proudly by the neat coils of black and white rope, glistening brass and rows of guns. Vulnerable though the wooden sides seem now, it was her tough live-oak frames that enabled her to survive the War of 1812 undefeated and win her her nickname. In 1997 she celebrated her 200th birthday, and every year on July 4 she takes a turn in the harbor, changing the side that faces the elements.

HIGHLIGHTS

- Museum: details of sailor's daily diet and duties
- U.S.S. *Constitution*: cramped quarters of crew

INFORMATION

- ✚ H3
- ✉ Charlestown Navy Yard
- ☎ Museum: 426-1812. Bunker Hill Pavilion: 241-7575
- 🕐 U.S.S. *Constitution*: normally 9:30–sunset. U.S.S. *Cassin Young*: 10–4. Museum: Mar–May 10–5; Jun–Labor Day 9–6; day after Labor Day–Nov 10–5; Dec–Feb 10–4. Bunker Hill Pavilion shows: Sep–May 9:30–4; Jun–Aug 9:30–5. Closed Dec–Mar
- 🍽 In the yard
- 🚇 North Station, then 10–15-minute walk
- 🚢 MBTA Water Shuttle from Long Wharf, MuSEAm Connection from Burroughs Wharf
- ♿ Ships and Museum wheelchair access
- 💵 Ships free. Museum moderate. Bunker Hill Pavilion moderate
- ❓ Tours U.S.S. *Cassin Young* lower decks. Tours Commandant's House. Museum shop

THE NORTH END & OLD NORTH CHURCH

HIGHLIGHTS

- Paul Revere House (➤ 45)
- Old North Church
- Copp's Hill Burying Ground (➤ 56)
- Feast day processions
- Italian groceries

INFORMATION

- ➕ d–c I–II/H3–4
- ✉ Bounded by Commercial Street and (roughly) the expressway
- 🍴 Plenty in and around Hanover and Salem streets
- 🚇 Haymarket, North Station, Aquarium, State
- ♿ Some hills
- ♿ Paul Revere House (➤ 45)

The North End is Boston's oldest and most spirited district. It's got a lot of history, a lot of character, and a lot of good places to eat.

Little Italy The North End today is separated from the rest of Boston by the J.F.K. Expressway, a.k.a. the Central Artery (until it's buried, take the walkway underneath). When the colonists arrived it was also all but cut off from Boston itself, surrounded by water at the end of a narrow peninsula. The colonists' eccentric street plan survives, but the only building from the 17th century is Paul Revere House (➤ 45). Once the élite had moved away to Beacon Hill in the early 1800s, the area played host to waves of immigrants, first the Irish, then East European and Portuguese, and finally Italians. It is the Italians who have given the area its current flavor, with Italian spoken in the streets, Italian pop music playing in the cafés, and lively weekend street festivals in July and August.

Old North Church St. Stephen's Church (➤ 56) in the main artery of Hanover Street faces Revere's statue (➤ 55) and, behind it, the tall white steeple of Old North Church. It was from Old North that Revere's signal was given to the patriots in Charlestown that the British were on their way to Lexington where, the next day, the first battle of the War of Independence took place. Up the hill from Old North is the Copp's Hill Burying Ground (➤ 56). From here wind down Snowhill and through the tall narrow streets to Salem Street and, perhaps, a treat from a *pasticceria*.

Old North steeple

PAUL REVERE HOUSE

*This rare example of early colonial archi-
tecture is all that remains of the 17th-
century settlement in today's North End.
Not only is it Boston's oldest building, it
was also the home of its most celebrated
son, Paul Revere.*

The early years The steep-gabled clapboard
house that we see today was built in about 1680.
Like most houses of the period, it had two
rooms on each of its two floors but the position-
ing of the main staircase at the side of the building, which makes the rooms larger than normal,
was unusual. By 1770, when the silversmith and
engraver Paul Revere (► 12) came to live here,
a number of significant alterations had been
made, notably the addition of a third floor and a
two-story extension at the back. The family
lived here during the Revolution, so it was from
here that Revere set out on that famous
midnight ride. In 1800, after the family sold the
house, it became a rooming house, with shops
and factory premises on the lower floor.
Threatened with demolition in 1902,
it was saved by Revere's great-grand-
son and, restored to something like its
origins, became a museum.

The house today The basic timber
skeleton of the house is the original,
but the exterior clapboarding, the
windows and most of what you see
inside are replacements. Go through
the kitchen into the living room,
furnished in period style. Upstairs,
the main bedroom is elegantly
furnished and would have doubled as
a parlor. In the other room, note the
ingenious folding bed and its traditional woven cover.

HIGHLIGHTS

● Revere's own account of his
ride
● Period furnishings

INFORMATION

✚ dII/H4
✉ 19 North Square
☎ 523-2338
◉ Nov–mid-Apr 9:30–4:15.
Mid-Apr–Oct 9:30–5:15.
Closed Mon Jan–Mar
🍴 Near by
Ⓜ Government Center, State,
Aquarium, Haymarket
♿ Wheelchair access lower
floor only
💷 Moderate
↔ Old North Church (► 44)
❓ Tours can be taken around
adjoining early Georgian
Pierce/Hichborn House

*Bronze bell cast by
Paul Revere*

23

NEW ENGLAND AQUARIUM

HIGHLIGHTS

- Giant OceanTank
- Watching tank divers
- The huge green sea turtle
- Whalewatch trip
- "Science at Sea" harbor trip

INFORMATION

- ✠ clll/J4
- ✉ Central Wharf
- ☎ 973-5200
- 🕐 1 Jul–Labor Day Mon, Tue, Fri 9–6; Wed, Thu 9–8; Sat, Sun, hols 9–7. Rest of year Mon–Wed, Fri 9–5; Thu 9–8 Sat, Sun, hols 9–6
- 🍽 On premises
- Ⓜ Aquarium
- 🚌 MuSEAm Connection (► 59)
- ♿ Good
- 💲 Expensive; Thu, summer Wed $1 off 4–7:30
- ❓ Whalewatch trips Apr–Oct ☎ 973-5281. Harbor tours Jul, Aug. Shop

Housing one of the largest aquatic collections in the world, this is a popular family excursion. Follow the spiral ramp that leads you around a vast cylindrical tank that swirls with myriad sea creatures of every imaginable size, shape, and color.

Exhibits Seals and sea otters cavort outside the entrance. Inside, the penguins hang out on the rocks at the base of the Giant Ocean Tank—until feeding time, that is. Follow the ramp past the Special Exhibit Gallery to the Thinking Gallery, where you can compare your hearing to that of a dolphin and your skeleton to that of a fish. The Freshwater Gallery has above- and below-surface views of a flooded Amazon forest complete with anaconda, alongside, by contrast, a New England trout stream. Eventually, you reach the top of the huge tank at the center of the Aquarium. At feeding times, approximately hourly, staff dive in, scattering squid for the bigger fish, jamming lettuce into the fiberglass coral reef for the angel fish, hand-feeding the sharks and giving the turtles their vitamin-enriched gelatin (to keep their shells hard). Notice how all the fish swim in the same direction, into the current set up by the filter, to get more oxygen.

Boat trips The *Voyager II* whalewatch trip is highly recommended, as is the "Science at Sea" harbor tour, when you can haul lobster traps and tow for plankton. This was the first aquarium to have a department devoted to aquatic conservation and a huge expansion project in the works at press time will help the Aquarium increase public awareness still further.

COMPUTER MUSEUM

For the younger generation this, the world's premier computer museum, is heaven. And even if you neither know how to program your VCR nor particularly want to, you will find the exhibits pretty compelling.

Computers and their uses The cornerstone exhibit is the Walk-through Computer. Children love to climb over the giant-sized keyboard and roll the massive trackball mouse to answer e-mail on a 12-ft. monitor. Walk right into the microprocessor, and try any of 30 hands-on activities that teach you how a CD-ROM or a modem works. You can use the PCs in the Tools & Toys exhibit to record your own music or make a cartoon. If you are able to get anywhere near a machine in the Best Kids Software room, you can have a look at the latest educational software (a popular spot for off-duty teachers). Swipe into The Networked Planet with a key card and then you can not only surf the Internet, you can buy and sell stock or learn about an ECG sensor. The air traffic display tracks every plane in the sky.

Evolution Older visitors recall the days when a computer almost filled a room—the People and Computers display traces today's personal computers back beyond that even, to 1930s punchcards. Robots and Other Smart Machines (meet R2-D2 from *Star Wars*) has 35 interactive stations at which you almost always will see 35 silent humans, totally absorbed in playing "Old MacDonald had a Farm" to a computer accompaniment, finding out how tall they are, or bargaining over a box of strawberries. If you can't take any more interacting, watch the show in the Robot Theater tracing robotics from old wind-up toys to the mechanical arms used in industry.

HIGHLIGHTS

- Walk-through Computer exhibit
- Tracking air traffic
- R2–D2
- Robot Theater show
- Educational games

INFORMATION

- J5
- 300 Congress Street, Museum Wharf
- 423-6758
- Winter Tue–Sun 10–5. Closed Mon except holidays and school vacations. Summer daily 10–6
- Very close
- South Station
- MuSEAm Connection (➤ 59)
- Good
- Expensive; half-price Sun 3–5
- Boston Tea Party Ship & Museum (➤ 52), Children's Museum (➤ 59)
- Multi-lingual tours. Shop

JOHN F. KENNEDY LIBRARY & MUSEUM

HIGHLIGHTS

- The building, its setting and views
- Introductory video
- Oval Office

DID YOU KNOW?

- The Library holds 8,400,000 JFK presidential papers

INFORMATION

- ✚ K9
- ✉ Columbia Point (Route 3/I–93 exit 15)
- ☎ 929-4523
- ⏰ 9–5
- 🍴 Café on premises
- 🚇 J. F. K./U.Mass., then free shuttle bus
- 🚢 Shuttle from Long Wharf, summer ☎ 929-4523
- ♿ Excellent
- 💷 Moderate
- ❓ Shop

"A man may die, nations may rise and fall, but an idea lives on", said the late president John F. Kennedy, whose life, leadership, and legacy are brilliantly evoked in this dramatic museum by the ocean.

The setting The presidential library and its museum constructed in 1979, are housed in an I. M. Pei building on Dorchester Bay, 4 miles southeast of downtown Boston. The building's two towers, of dark glass and smooth white concrete, command fine views of the city, the bay and Boston Harbor Islands. The lawns, dune grass, and wild roses in the grounds recall the Kennedy summer home on Cape Cod. In summer the ferry from Long Wharf is an excursion in itself.

The New Museum An introductory film covers Kennedy's early years from childhood to the 1960 presidential campaign. Re-created settings include the White House corridors and the Oval Office, complete with the rocking chair J. F. K. used for his bad back and, on his desk, the coconut inscribed "HELP" that led to his rescue after his naval ship sank in the Pacific. Videos cover significant events such as the Cuban Missile Crisis, the space program and the assassination. There are family photographs and other memorabilia.

The Presidential Library This is one of nine presidential libraries holding the papers of nine of the US presidents since Herbert Hoover. The Presidential Library System allows presidents to establish a library and museum where ever they choose. The JFK Library is near his mother's home.

BOSTON's
best

NEIGHBORHOODS

See Top 25 Sights for
BACK BAY (➤ 33)
BEACON HILL (➤ 35)
THE NORTH END (➤ 44)

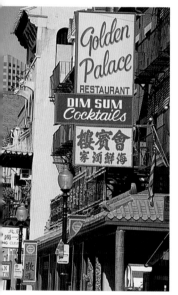

Chinatown

CAMBRIDGE

Cambridge is a town with its own character on the other side of the Charles River, but it is so accessible it feels like a neighborhood of Boston. Home to Harvard, M.I.T. and 28,000 students from all around the world, Cambridge is nothing if not vibrant. Life centers on several "squares" or districts. There is lots for visitors to see and do in and around Harvard Square (➤ 25, 26), both by day and by night. Inman Square, Central Square, and Porter Square all have a lively night scene with diverse international restaurants. Kendall Square is M.I.T.'s home, close to the river and the Cambridgeside Galleria mall.

CHINATOWN AND THE THEATER DISTRICT

Bounded by Washington Street, Essex Street, Kneeland Street, and the Central Artery, between the Theater District and Financial District, Boston's Chinatown is not large but offers a real taste of Chinese daily life and Far Eastern cuisine. The principal artery is Beach Street, with the traditional gateway at the eastern end. With the Theater District on the other side of Washington Street, Chinatown is handy for late eating, but be careful—the area borders the Combat Zone, the rapidly shrinking red-light district along lower Washington Street.

DOWNTOWN CROSSING

Immediately east of Boston Common is a mostly pedestrians-only shopping area that encompasses part of Washington Street and the streets that link it to Tremont Street. Department stores Filene's and Macy's (formerly Jordan Marsh) are here, as well as Filene's Basement (➤ 77) and numerous fashion stores (➤ 70).

FENWAY

Art and sports meet here with the Museum of Fine Arts (➤ 28) and the Isabella Stewart Gardner Museum (➤ 27) on one side of the Back Bay Fens public park, and Fenway Park, home of the Red Sox and the Green Monster, on the other.

FINANCIAL DISTRICT AND LEATHER DISTRICT

The Financial District has some interesting buildings (▶ 54). Between there and Chinatown, cornered by Kneeland Street and Atlantic Avenue, is the Leather District, a piece of 19th-century industrial Boston whose redbrick buildings once serviced the shoe industry. Today they are offices, small industrial premises, and the occasional wine bar.

THE OLD WEST END AND GOVERNMENT CENTER

Though not exciting as a district, the old West End has the FleetCenter, home to the Celtics and Bruins, next to North Station, in a fairly desolate area cut by a twin-level expressway. Beside the Charles river lies the granite Old Jail and hidden in Mass. General Hospital is the Bulfinch Pavilion, where ether was first used as an anesthetic.

THE SOUTH END

First occupied by musicians and teachers in the 1850s and 1860s, the South End had taken a social nose-dive by the end of the 19th century but is now very much back in favor with young professionals. It is a lively residential area whose elegant bowfronted terraces, many profusely decorated with balustrades and windowboxes, line leafy streets and squares. Running through the middle is Tremont Street, where local stores are punctuated by eating places. There is a broad ethnic mix here and a strong gay element. Not to be confused with South Boston, farther to the east, the South End lies between Huntington Ave. and the Expressway. See panel for a walk.

WATERFRONT

The Waterfront, immediately east of Faneuil Hall Marketplace, the North End, and the Financial District, is currently being ravaged by the construction work that will eventually bury the Central Artery. Its old granite wharf buildings that once bustled with commercial activity are now luxury condos or offices overlooking trendy yacht havens. Boat trips leave from Long Wharf, the Aquarium, and Rowes Wharf (▶ 19, 46). There is a walkway along to Museum Wharf (for the Computer and Children's museums, ▶ 47, 59), and there are several seafood restaurants (▶ 64).

Ironwork typical of the South End

A South End stroll

From Copley or Back Bay T, walk south down Dartmouth Avenue, over Columbus Avenue. Zig-zag through Lawrence, Appleton, and Gray streets. Take Clarendon Street down to Tremont Street. Go right and left into Union Park. Go right (west) along Shawmut Avenue, right onto Upton or Pembroke Street. Left at Tremont, right onto Rutland or Concord Square. Cut back across Columbus Ave. and up West Newton St. to Huntington Ave. and the Pru T.

HOUSES, MUSEUMS & GALLERIES

Brookline sightseeing

Coolodge Corner has the **J. F. K. National Historic Site** ➕ B5 ✉ 83 Beals Street ☎ 566-7937 🕐 Mid-May–mid Oct Wed–Sun, 10–4:30 🚇 Coolidge Corner (Green Line C)

The **Frederick Law Olmsted National Historic Site** (➤ 57) has landscaped gardens. ➕ C8 ✉ 99 Warren Street ☎ 566-1689 🕐 Fri–Sun 10–4:30 🚇 Brookline Hills (Green Line D) then ¾-mile walk.

The Museum of Transportation is in Larz Anderson Park. ➕ A10 ✉ 15 Newton Street, Brookline ☎ 522-6140 🕐 Wed–Sun 10–5 🚇 Cleveland Circle (Green Line C), then Bus 51 (not Sun)

J. F. K.'s birthplace, Brookline

See Top 25 Sights for
COMPUTER MUSEUM (➤ 47)
HARRISON GRAY OTIS HOUSE (➤ 37)
HARVARD UNIVERSITY MUSEUMS (➤ 26)
ISABELLA STEWART GARDNER MUSEUM (➤ 27)
JOHN F. KENNEDY LIBRARY & MUSEUM (➤ 48)
LONGFELLOW HOUSE (➤ 24)
MUSEUM OF FINE ARTS (➤ 28)
MUSEUM OF SCIENCE (➤ 34)
PAUL REVERE HOUSE (➤ 45)
U.S.S. CONSTITUTION MUSEUM (➤ 43)

BOSTON TEA PARTY SHIP & MUSEUM

Board a replica Tea Party ship, stick a plastic feather in your hair, boo the Brits and maybe get to throw a styrofoam tea chest into the sea—but be aware that there are other ways of learning about this significant event (➤ 40).

➕ H5 ✉ Congress Street Bridge ☎ 338-1773 🕐 9–5; summer 9–6. Closed Dec 1–mid-Mar 🍴 Near by 🚇 South Station ♿ No wheelchair access to boat 🎟 Moderate

CHILDREN'S MUSEUM (➤ 59)

GIBSON HOUSE MUSEUM

An 1860 Back Bay family home, virtually untouched. Complete with creaky stairs, worn carpets, and a wonderful collection of Victoriana, it is a fragile treasure worth fitting into your schedule if you can. Afternoon tours only. ➕ G5 ✉ 137 Beacon Street ☎ 267-6338 🕐 For tours only at 1, 2, 3PM May–Oct Wed–Sun. Nov–Apr Wed–Sun, Sun. Also by appointment 🍴 Near by 🚇 Arlington ♿ No wheelchair access 🎟 Moderate

INSTITUTE OF CONTEMPORARY ART (ICA)

An exhibition, film, and performance space housed in a 19th-century police and fire station. No permanent collection, but whatever's on is likely to be innovative. ➕ F5 ✉ 955 Boylston Street (at Hereford Street) ☎ 267-5152 🕐 Wed–Sun 12–5; Thu until 9 🍴 Restaurant next door 🚇 Hynes Convention Center/ICA 🎟 Moderate; free Thu 5–9

M.I.T. MUSEUMS

The main M.I.T. exhibition space has a unique collection of holograms, including that one of a woman winking and blowing a kiss at you. It is also home to the Hall of Hacks, featuring M.I.T. student pranks (on display is the police car found on top of the M.I.T. Dome in May 1994). Here too you can see some of Harold "Doc" Edgerton's sequential photos of a balloon bursting. The Hart Nautical Collections, in the main campus, cover the technical side of naval architecture with exquisite ship models.

Main center ✚ E4 ✉ 265 Massachusetts Avenue, Cambridge
☎ 253-4444 🕐 Tue–Fri 10–5; Sat–Sun 12–5 🚇 Central 🚌 1 to Necco Candy stop 🎟 Cheap
Hart Nautical Gallery ✚ E4 ✉ Building 5, 77 Massachusetts Avenue
☎ 253-5942 🕐 Daily 9–8 🚇 Kendall 🎟 Free

AFRICAN MEETING HOUSE/MUSEUM OF AFRO-AMERICAN HISTORY

A museum dedicated to the history of African Americans in Boston is housed in the African Meeting House, built in 1806 and the oldest surviving black church building in the U.S. Originally a center for social and political activity, it is now a focal point on the Black Heritage Trail, a walking tour of pre-Civil War Beacon Hill sites including Smith Court Residences and Abiel Smith School.

✚ B3 ✉ 46 Joy Street ☎ 742-1854 🕐 Daily 10–4 🍴 No
🚇 Bowdoin 🎟 Gallery moderate; Meeting House free

NICHOLS HOUSE MUSEUM

One of Boston's earliest Federal-style houses, this elegant four-story Beacon Hill house was built by Charles Bulfinch (▶ 12, 35) in 1804 and is furnished with Nichols family art and antiques. The informative guide is also talkative—worth noting if time is short.

✚ B3 ✉ 55 Mount Vernon Street ☎ 227-6993
🕐 May–Oct, Tue–Sat 12–5. Nov–Dec and Feb–Apr Mon, Wed, Sat 12–5; tours 🍴 No 🚇 Park Street 🎟 Moderate

SPORTS MUSEUM OF NEW ENGLAND

Climb a simulated rock wall, do the Boston Marathon in a wheelchair, see a cut-away New England bowling alley—or just wallow in the sports memorabilia. The museum is well worth the trip to Lowell (▶ 21).

✚ Off map to northwest ✉ 25 Shattuck St., Lowell
☎ (617) 787-7678 🕐 Tue–Sun 10–5:30. Sun 11–7
🍴 Near by 🚇 MBTA train to Lowell 🎟 Moderate

Waxwork of baseball player Carl Yastrzemski in the Sports Museum

BUILDINGS: LATE 19TH CENTURY & 20TH CENTURY

Downtown, near State Street

M.I.T. Buildings

M.I.T. has some impressive modern architecture. You are free to wander around the campus. Seek out Eero Saarinen's serene round chapel (1955), near the Student Center on Mass Ave. Overlooking the river near by, the student dorm Baker House (1947) is by Finnish architect Alvar Aalto, while on and near Ames Street the low Wiesner and the tall Green buildings are the work of I. M. Pei (1985, 1964).

➕ E4 ✉ Massachusetts Avenue, Memorial Drive, Ames Street 🚇 Kendall

See Top 25 Sights for
**BOSTON PUBLIC
LIBRARY (► 31)
JOHN HANCOCK
TOWER (► 30)
TRINITY CHURCH (► 32)**

AMES AND SEARS BUILDINGS

The highly decorative 14-story 1889 Ames Building at the back of the Old State House dominated the skyline until the Custom House Tower was built. The nearby Sears Building (1868) was the first in the city to have an elevator.
➕ dIII/H4 ✉ 1 Court Street 🚇 State

CUSTOM HOUSE TOWER

The square clock tower (1915) is a Boston landmark and at 30 stories was for a long while the city's tallest skyscraper. It's only when you see the building at street level that you realize how ridiculous it looks stuck on the roof of the original Custom House, built in 1847 like a temple, in Greek Revival style. The clock faces are notorious for showing different times.
➕ dIII/H4 ✉ State Street 🚇 State

IN AND AROUND POST OFFICE SQUARE

On the corner of Water and Congress, note the elaborate façade of the art deco US Post Office and Court House (1931). Next to it is Arts & Crafts No. 79 Milk Street, with green and white detailing at roof level, and at the south end of the square is the striking New England Telephone building. In Franklin Street find good art deco metalwork on the exterior walls of the State Street Trust Building at 75, and in the foyer of State Street Bank, No. 225. Worthy of mention, too, are the stepped-back United Shoe Machinery building (1929), 138–164 Federal Street at High Street, and the 1928 Batterymarch Building at 60 Batterymarch Street.

WINTHROP BUILDING

Boston's first all steel-framed skyscraper (1894).
➕ dIV/H5 ✉ 7 Water Street, between Washington Street and Post Office Square 🚇 State

STATUES, MONUMENTS & SCULPTURES

SAM ADAMS
Anne Whitney's (1880) portrayal of the defiant revolutionary leader, in front of Faneuil Hall.
➕ dIII/H4 ✉ Congress Street 🚇 State

BUNKER HILL MONUMENT
The Charlestown skyline is punctuated by this plain gray obelisk commemorating the revolutionary Battle of Bunker Hill. Climb 274 steps for good views.
➕ H2 ✉ Monument Square, Charlestown ☎ 242-5641 🕐 Daily 9–4:30 🚢 Long Wharf to Charlestown 🚇 Community College 💲 Free

JAMES CURLEY
A colorful Boston Irish mayor, Curley comes seated and standing (Lloyd Lillie, 1980).
➕ dIII/H4 ✉ North/Union Street 🚇 State

MAKE WAY FOR DUCKLINGS (► 59)

M.I.T. SCULPTURES
On the campus are two Henry Moore reclining figure pieces (1963, 1976), Alexander Calder's black steel *The Big Sail* (1965), and Michael Heizer's pink granite *Guennette* (1977).
➕ E4 ✉ Memorial Drive 🕐 Daily 🚇 Kendall 💲 Free

NEW ENGLAND HOLOCAUST MEMORIAL
Six glass towers, the poignant work of Stanley Saitowitz (1995), one for each Nazi death camp. Etched numerals represent the Holocaust's 6 million victims.
➕ dIII/H4 ✉ Union Street 🚇 State

PAUL REVERE
A bronze equestrian statue (1940) of the legendary figure (► 12) by Cyrus Dallin.
➕ dII/H4 ✉ Paul Revere Mall, North End 🚇 State, Aquarium, North Station

ROBERT GOULD SHAW MONUMENT
A bronze battle frieze by Augustus Saint-Gaudens (1897). Shaw, depicted in the film *Glory*, led the Union's first black regiment off to battle in the Civil War. Here, for the first time, blacks were portrayed by a white artist as individuals.
➕ bIV/G4 ✉ Beacon Street, facing State House 🚇 Park

Art on the T
MBTA (Massachusetts Bay Transportation Authority) has an enlightened policy of installing works of art in its subway stations. Keep an eye out, for example, for the layered hands sculpture and the ceramic mural in Park Street station, the granite benches placed randomly on the platforms at Downtown Crossing or the multi-colored "Omphaios" sculpture outside Harvard Square station.

Statue of Paul Revere

PLACES OF WORSHIP & BURIAL GROUNDS

See Top 25 Sights for
CHRISTIAN SCIENCE CENTER (► 29)
OLD NORTH CHURCH (► 44)
OLD SOUTH MEETING HOUSE (► 40)
TRINITY CHURCH (► 32)

AFRICAN MEETING HOUSE (► 53)

Mount Auburn Cemetery, Cambridge

A little out of the way, but a beautiful place. It was built in 1831 as the country's first rural garden cemetery and is still very popular with bird and plant lovers. If it's a nice day you could walk from Longfellow's House (► 24). Longfellow now rests here, as does artist Winslow Homer.

➕ 2B ✉ Mt. Auburn Street, Cambridge ☎ 547-7105
🕐 Daily 🚇 Harvard, then walk or Watertown bus

Park Street Church

COPP'S HILL BURYING GROUND
Up on top of an old Native American look-out point in the North End, the rows of carved skulls have good all-round views. Puritans Increase and Cotton Mather are buried here.
➕ dl/H3 ✉ Hull Street 🕐 Daily 🚇 North Station

KING'S CHAPEL AND BURYING GROUND
This was built as an Anglican church in 1687 on the orders of King James II, to the indignation of the Puritan colonists. In the town's earliest (1630) burial ground lie two *Mayflower* passengers and John Winthrop, first governor of Massachusetts.
➕ dIV/H4 ✉ Tremont/School streets 🚇 Park

OLD GRANARY BURYING GROUND
If you can take in only one burial ground, make it this one. Dating back to 1660, it's the leafy resting place of many of the big names you keep coming across—Paul Revere, James Otis, John Hancock, Samuel Adams, Peter Faneuil. A board tells you about the wonderful carvings on the headstones.
➕ dIV/H5 ✉ 88 Tremont Street 🕐 Daily 🚇 Park

PARK STREET CHURCH
Notable as much for its tall white steeple as for William Lloyd Garrison's first anti-slavery speech made in 1829. "America the Beautiful" was first sung here in 1831.
➕ dIV/H5 ✉ 1 Park Street 🕐 Jul–Aug daily 🚇 Park

ST. STEPHEN'S CHURCH
Of the dozen churches Charles Bulfinch designed for post-Independence Boston, this is the only one still standing (1804). Its redbrick tower contrasts with the wide, white-painted Federal interior.
➕ E15 ✉ 41 Hanover Street 🕐 Daily 🚇 State

PARKS & RETREATS

See Top 25 Sights for
THE PUBLIC GARDEN (▶ 36)
BOSTON COMMON (▶ 36)

ARNOLD ARBORETUM
This is a rolling hilly park that's well worth the trip to the suburbs. Designed by Frederick Law Olmsted as part of the Emerald Necklace (see panel).
⊞ B10 ⊠ 125 Arborway, Jamaica Plain ☎ 524-1718 🚇 Orange line to Forest Hills 🎟 Free

BACK BAY FENS
The Back Bay Fens was the first of Olmsted's string of parks (see panel). Tall rushes line the Muddy River banks behind the M.F.A., and people stroll through the willows, or sit in the Rose Garden.
⊞ E6 ⊠ The Fenway/Park Drive 🚇 Museum, Hynes

BOSTON HARBOR ISLANDS
Dotted over 50 square miles of Boston Harbor are more than 30 islands. Take a ferry (45 minutes) to George's Island. Go for a walk or visit Civil War Fort Warren, or catch a shuttle to one of the other islands. All have beaches and nature trails.
⊞ clll/J4 ⊠ Bay State Cruise Company, 67 Long Wharf ☎ 723-7800 🕐 Ferry to George's Island May–Oct; inter-island shuttle end June through Labor Day 🎟 Water and food available only on George's 🚇 Aquarium 🎟 Moderate; inter-island shuttle free

CHARLES RIVER: ESPLANADE AND BOAT TOURS
A favorite for rollerblading, jogging, sunbathing and more (▶ 58 Biking, Boating); free summer concerts in Hatch Memorial Shell (▶ 78). Charles Riverboat Tours leave from the Cambridge side near the Science Museum.
Esplanade ⊞ F5 ⊠ Storrow Memorial Drive/Embankment Road 🚇 Charles/MGH
Riverboat Tours ⊞ b1 ⊠ 100 CambridgeSide ☎ 621-3001 🕐 Apr–Nov daily 🚇 Science Park

The Emerald Necklace

So called because it resembles a string of beads, Boston's interconnecting chain of parks was designed in 1895, when such things were a novel idea, by America's first landscape architect, Frederick Law Olmsted. The gardens of Commonwealth Avenue link Boston Common and the Public Garden with the Back Bay Fens. From here it is possible to walk along the reed-fringed Riverway to Olmsted Park and on to Jamaica Pond, a popular spot for fishing and boating. Arnold Arboretum (see left) is ½ mile away and then there's Franklin Park, with a zoo (▶ 59).

Autumn colors on the Charles River Esplanade

SPORTS & OUTDOOR ACTIVITIES

Sailing on the Charles River

The major venues

Fenway Park 🚑 E6 ✉ 24
Yawkey Way ☎ 267-8661
🍴 Near by 🚇 Kenmore
Square

FleetCenter 🚑 Cl/H4
✉ 150 Causeway Street
☎ Tickets: 624 1000.
Tours: 624 1518 🕐 Tours daily
10–4:30 🍴 Sports café
🚇 North Station

Tickets are also available through
Ticketmaster ☎ 931-2000 or
931-2787 or at BosTix stalls in
Faneuil Hall Marketplace and
Copley Square.

BASEBALL/FENWAY TOURS
The beloved Boston Red Sox play at Fenway Park from April to October. Aged, cramped and idiosyncratic, Fenway is famous for its Green Monster—the mighty left field wall.

BASKETBALL
The Boston Celtics play October–May in the FleetCenter.

BIKING, ROLLERBLADING, AND JOGGING
The Esplanade is always popular. On spring and summer Sundays Memorial Drive, on the Cambridge side of the river, is closed to vehicles, so you can walk, cycle or rollerblade along one bank, cross on any bridge and return on the other. For bike and rollerblade rental ▶ 74, panel.

BOATING
Canoes, kayaks, and sailing dinghies can be rented at the Charles River Esplanade.

THE BOSTON MARATHON
Started in 1897, the first marathon in the U.S., and the world's oldest annual event, this 26.2-mile run (Hopkinton to Copley Square) takes place the third Monday in April.

FLEETCENTER TOURS
Daily tours start in a room dedicated to the late, lamented Boston Garden.

HEAD OF THE CHARLES REGATTA
Thousands come, often with picnics, for this major international rowing event in October.

ICE HOCKEY
The NHL's illustrious Boston Bruins play at FleetCenter (Oct–Apr).
The Beanpot, an inter-collegiate tournament, is in early February.

SKATING
In winter join the ritual skating on the pond in the Public Garden or on Frog Pond on Boston Common. Skates for rent at both. Alternatively, there is an indoor rink in the North End.
Rink, Commercial Street, North End ☎ 523 9327

THINGS FOR CHILDREN TO SEE & DO

Many a child loves the street performers in Faneuil Marketplace, and there are souvenir stores, candy stalls and food stands. Harvard Square, too, has plenty of street entertainment. Whale watching trips, Duck Tours and Swan Boats (▶ 46, 19, 36) are popular, and you might take your youngsters up to the John Hancock Observatory and/or Prudential Skywalk (▶ 30).

BOSTON HARBOR ISLANDS (▶ 57)

CHILDREN'S MUSEUM
Squirt water jets at model boats, stretch a gigantic bubble, play grocery store with life-size products—or just have fun in the playspace.
🚇 J5 ✉ 300 Congress Street, Museum Wharf ☎ 426-8855 🕐 Mid-Jun through Labor Day daily 10–5; Fri until 9. Sep–Jun closed Mon except school and public holidays 🍴 McDonald's adjoins 🚉 South Station 🎫 Expensive; but Fri 5–9 $1

FRANKLIN PARK ZOO
Wander through an African Tropical Forest, stroke small animals at the Children's Zoo, visit the lions, then picnic in the park's hills and meadows.
🚇 E10 ✉ 1 Franklin Park Road ☎ 442-2002 🕐 Daily 🍴 Café or picnic 🚉 Forest Hills (Orange Line) then bus 16 to main entrance 🎫 Moderate; under 4 free

M.I.T. MUSEUM (▶ 52)

PUPPET THEATER
(▶ 80–81)

MAKE WAY FOR DUCKLINGS
Every small Bostonian knows the mother duck and ducklings in the Public Garden, a bronze sculpture based on Robert McCloskey's famous book. The same artist, Nancy Schon, created the hare and tortoise who mark the spot where the Boston Marathon ends in Copley Square.

MuSEAm Connection/water shuttle

A fun way to get between several harborside places that children enjoy is the MuSEAm Connection, a boat shuttle that operates in summer between U.S.S. *Constitution*, the Aquarium and Museum Wharf for the Computer Museum, the Children's Museum and the Boston Tea Party Ship.
🕐 End May–Labor Day daily 10–5 (hourly). Sep–mid-Oct Sat, Sun 🎫 Moderate

Make way for ducklings!

FREEBIES & CHEAPIES

A Boston Pops concert in the Hatch Shell

Places of interest with free entry

African Meeting House (➤ 53)

Boston Athenaeum (➤ 39)

Boston Public Library (➤ 31)

Christian Science Center Mapparium and Mother Church (➤ 29)

Commonwealth Museum, history and people of Massachusetts ✉ 220 Morrissey Boulevard, Columbia Point ☎ 727-9268 🕙 Mon–Fri 9–5, Sat 9–3

Faneuil Hall (➤ 42)

Harvard University Museums on Saturday mornings (➤ 26)

Massachusetts State House (➤ 38)

Trinity Church (and free organ recitals Fri 12:15) (➤ 32)

U.S.S. *Constitution* (➤ 43)

Street entertainment

Harvard Square in Cambridge and Faneuil Hall Marketplace in Boston are both excellent places to catch street performers and for people-watching.

ADMISSION TO MUSEUMS, GALLERIES, ETC.

Several places offer reduced-price or free entry at certain times. The Museum of Fine Arts is pay-as-you-wish Wednesday 4–9:45. Harvard University Museums are free Saturday 10–12. The ICA is free after 5. Admission to the Children's Museum is $1 Friday 5–9, to the Computer Museum half price Sunday 3–5, and to the Aquarium it's cheaper after 4 every Wednesday and on Thursday in summer.

FESTIVALS

From summer festivals in the Italian North End and 4th of July fireworks displays on the Esplanade to Christmas tree-lighting ceremonies at the Prudential Center and the First Night celebrations on New Year's Eve, there's nearly always some free event going on. Check the *Boston Globe* or *Phoenix*.

MUSICAL ENTERTAINMENT

The ever-popular Boston Pops orchestra holds free concerts in July in the Hatch Memorial Shell on the Esplanade (➤ 78–79). Concerts at the New England Conservatory are free (Jan–Mar) (➤ 78). The Boston Symphony Orchestra has inexpensive open rehearsals. See the *Boston Globe* or *Phoenix*.

PARKS AND OPEN SPACES

It doesn't cost anything to enjoy the places described under Parks and Retreats (➤ 57). The Charles River Esplanade, Boston Common, and the Public Garden are year-round favorites.

BOSTON
where to...

THE BEST OF BOSTON

Prices

Approximate prices for a two-course meal for one person with one drink:

$ =   up to $18.

$$ = $18–35

$$$ = over $35

Slipped in amongst all the expensive restaurants here—Boston's very best—are two or three slightly less costly perennial favorites.

AMBROSIA ON HUNTINGTON ($$$)

The unconventional menu is French with a twist of Asian (lamb rack in Indonesian tomato sauce), the decor modern.
➕ F6 ✉ 116 Huntington Avenue ☎ 247-2400 🕐 Lunch Mon–Sat, dinner daily 🚇 Prudential

AUJOURD'HUI ($$$)

Known as much for the service as the food, this is one of Boston's very best formal restaurants. The elegant, comfortable dining room has a view of the Public Garden. The chef's complex presentations and unusual combinations don't come cheap, but the overall experience is as close to perfect as it gets. Formal dress.
➕ G5 ✉ Four Seasons Hotel, 200 Boylston Street ☎ 451-1392 🕐 Lunch/brunch, dinner 🚇 Arlington

BIBA ($$$)

Perhaps Boston's most famous chef, Lydia Shire is revered for her rich and satisfying personal style of cooking. On the unusually arranged menu—dishes are listed by principal ingredients rather than by category—offal plays a special role. Good view of the Public Garden from the upstairs room. Less formal eating at the bar downstairs.
➕ G5 ✉ 272 Boylston Street ☎ 426-7878 🕐 Lunch, dinner 🚇 Arlington

CAFE BUDAPEST ($$$)

Romantic Hungarian restaurant in something of a time-warp, violins and all. Good service. Soups are a specialty. Dressy.
➕ F57 ✉ Copley Square Hotel, 90 Exeter Street ☎ 266-1979/734 3388 🕐 Lunch, dinner 🚇 Copley

CHEZ HENRI ($$$)

French/Cuban, extremely trendy. Service can be tardy, but is well worth the wait. Look out for such specialties as frogs' legs and paella. Food is uniformly wonderful, sourced from a variety of styles.
➕ C3 ✉ 1 Shepard Street ☎ 354-89808 🕐 Closed Mon 🚇 Harvard Square

DURGIN PARK ($$)

One of the oldest dining rooms in the U.S. The roast beef melts in the mouth and there's hard-to-find traditional fare like Indian pudding (made from cornmeal, milk and molasses). Crowded and very informal—and the waiters make a thing of being rude. No reservations.
➕ dIII/H4 ✉ Faneuil Hall Marketplace, 340 North Market ☎ 227-2038 🕐 Daily from 11:30 🚇 State

THE ELEPHANT WALK ($$)

Intriguing Cambodian and French food. Popular with Cambridge students and young trendies.
➕ E2 ✉ 70 Union Sq,

Somerville ☎ 623-9939
🅒 Lunch Mon–Sat, dinner daily
🅢 Central Square (then 1 mile)

GRILL 23 & BAR ($$$)
Delicious steak and
seafood and attentive
service in a beautiful
dining room. Popular,
noisy and occasionally too
smoky.
➕ G5 ✉ 161 Berkeley Street
(at Stuart Street) ☎ 542-2255
🅒 Dinner only 🅢 Arlington

**HAMERSLEY'S
BISTRO ($$$)**
Excellent American-
French cooking in a
pleasant, informal setting.
Refreshingly simple
preparations.
➕ G6 ✉ 553 Tremont Street
(at Clarendon) ☎ 423-2700
🅒 Dinner only 🅢 Back Bay

JULIEN ($$$)
Very French, very formal,
very pricey, but the food is
superb. Not for those
easily intimidated by the
rituals of fine dining or
those with an aversion to
butter.
➕ dIV/H4 ✉ Le Meridien
Hotel, 250 Franklin Street
☎ 451-1900 🅒 Lunch (not
Sat), dinner. Closed Sun 🅢 State

L'ESPALIER ($$$)
Another of Boston's
formal, pricey restaurants,
L'Espalier offers superb
contemporary fare in an
elegant, comfortable Back
Bay house.
➕ F5 ✉ 30 Gloucester Street
☎ 262-3023 🅒 Dinner only.
Closed Sun 🅢 Prudential, Hynes
Convention Center

**LOCKE-OBER CAFE
($$$)**
A Boston institution, the
Edwardian-style dining
room was originally a
gentlemen's club, and still
feels like one. The menu
is old-fashioned, but
competently executed.
Definitely no jeans.
➕ cIV/H5 ✉ 3 Winter Place
☎ 542-1340 🅒 From 11:30
weekdays. Dinner only Sat, Sun
🅢 Downtown Crossing

**MAISON ROBERT
($$$/$$)**
As French as the name,
the food at Maison Robert
is good, if old-fashioned;
the wine list impressive, if
expensive, and the dining
room pleasingly formal. A
Boston mainstay.
➕ cIV/H4 ✉ 45 School Street
☎ 227-3370 🅒 Lunch, dinner
🅢 State, Park

OLIVES ($$)
Imaginative
Mediterranean-
influenced cooking.
Flavors are bold and
portions are huge.
Chef/owner Todd English
has become a gossip-
column favorite.
➕ H3 ✉ 10 City Square,
Charlestown ☎ 242-1999
🅒 Dinner only. Closed Sun, Mon
🅢 North Station

**RITZ-CARLTON DINING
ROOM ($$$)**
Traditional dining under
the chandeliers of the
elegant second-floor room
overlooking the Public
Garden. Outstanding
service and food. Formal
dress de rigueur.
➕ G5 ✉ 15 Arlington Street
☎ 536-5700 🅒 Dinner daily,
brunch Sun 🅢 Arlington

Dining with a view

BAY TOWER ROOM ($$$)
Look down on the city and harbor
from 33 floors up. New American
cuisine.
➕ dIII/H4 ✉ 60 State Street
☎ 723-1666 🅒 Dinner.
Closed Sun 🅢 State

**JOE'S AMERICAN BAR &
GRILL ($–$$)**
Regional American dishes right on
the water's edge.
➕ cIII/J4 ✉ 100 Atlantic
Avenue ☎ 367-8700
🅢 Aquarium

SEASONS ($$)
Luxury rooftop dining room offers
New American cuisine and views
over Faneuil Hall Marketplace.
➕ dIII/H4 ✉ Bostonian Hotel,
9 Blackstone Street ☎ 523-
3600 🅒 Lunch Mon–Fri, dinner
daily 🅢 State

TOP OF THE HUB
The highest (if far from the best)
dining room in Boston, on the
52nd floor of the Prudential Tower.
The night-time views are superb.
➕ F6 ✉ Prudential Center,
Huntington Avenue ☎ 536-
1775 🅒 Lunch, dinner
🅢 Prudential

See also Aujourd'hui, Biba,
Anthony's Pier 4, Barking Crab
(► 64); Davio's (► 65).

63

SEAFOOD

For Landlubbers only: how to eat a lobster

1 Put the bib on

2 Break the claws off

3 Use the nutcracker to open them

4 Bend the back until the tailpiece splits off

5 Break the flippers off the tail

6 Push the meat out of the tail with the thin fork

7 Pull the back out of the body. You may not want to eat the liver

8 Crack open the rest of the body sideways (the best meat is here)

9 Suck the meat out of the little claw

ANTHONY'S PIER 4 ($$)

Big, busy restaurant on the Fish Pier where anyone who's anyone has eaten. Anything that swims comes grilled, baked, fried, or blackened. Reservations (and jackets) advisable.
🚇 J5 ✉ 140 Northern Avenue ☎ 423-6363 🕐 From 11:30 🚉 South Station

BARKING CRAB ($)

A rough and ready old clam shack where you can eat your lobster crabcakes indoors or *al fresco*, with a view of downtown Boston across the water. Be prepared for noise, crowds, a wait and some fun.
🚇 J5 ✉ 88 Sleeper Street (Northern Avenue) ☎ 426-2722 🚉 South Station

THE FAMOUS ATLANTIC FISH CO ($$)

Back Bay seafood diner which also serves meat and pasta. Good clam chowder with fresh-baked bread. Note the ceiling fan mechanism.
🚇 F5 ✉ 777 Boylston Street ☎ 267-4000 🕐 From 11:30 🚉 Copley

JIMMY'S HARBORSIDE ($$)

Fine old institution with good, solid fish and steak dishes, sometimes over-cooked, and a first-class wine list. Excellent waterfront views.
🚇 J5 ✉ 242 Northern Avenue ☎ 423-1000 🕐 From noon; Sun dinner only 🚉 South Station

LEGAL SEA FOODS ($$)

Very popular seafood chain serving straight-forward but reliably good fish dishes. Makes a decent clam chowder. Slightly rushed service.
✉ Prudential Center; Copley Place, Park Plaza Hotel, 35 Columbus Avenue; 5 Cambridge Center, Kendall Square, Cambridge; and other locations ☎ 426-4444; 864-3400 🕐 Hours vary 🚉 Prudential; Arlington; Kendall

SKIPJACK'S ($$)

Well-prepared fish in comfortable surroundings. If you don't want lobster, a specialty, try blackened tuna sashimi.
🚇 F5 ✉ 199 Clarendon Street ☎ 536-3500 🕐 From 11:00. Sun jazz brunch 🚉 Copley

TURNER FISHERIES ($$)

The acclaimed seafood restaurant in the Westin Hotel prides itself on its clam chowder, so this has to be your benchmark. Good Sunday brunch. Live jazz next door.
🚇 F5 ✉ The Westin Hotel, Copley Place, 10 Huntington Avenue ☎ 424-7425 🕐 From 11:30, Sun brunch from 11 🚉 Copley

UNION OYSTER HOUSE ($$)

Said to be the oldest restaurant in the U.S., right on the Freedom Trail. Try the Boston scrod, a local favorite.
🚇 dIII/J4 ✉ 41 Union Street ☎ 227 2750 🕐 From 11 🚉 State

Also ➤ 63, Grill 23 & Bar.

ITALIAN & MEDITERRANEAN

ANAGO BISTRO ($$$)
In its new Back Bay home in the Lenox Hotel, Anago serves contemporary food as strongly flavored as ever, using fresh ingredients.
➕ F5 ✉ Lenox Hotel, 710 Boylston Street ☎ 536-5300 🕐 Lunch, dinner Ⓣ Copley

ARTÙ ($)
Country-style Italian cooking in the North End. Friendly, informal atmosphere. Try chicken layered with eggplant and mozarella, and leave room for dessert. Also at 89 Charles Street, Beacon Hill.
➕ dII/H4 ✉ 6 Prince Street ☎ 742-4336 🕐 From 9AM Ⓣ Haymarket

CANTINA ITALIANA ($)
A relaxed, comfortable North End eatery that serves excellent food from several regions of Italy.
➕ dII/H4 ✉ 346 Hanover Street ☎ 723-4577 🕐 Mon–Fri from 4, Sat Sun from noon Ⓣ Haymarket

DALI ($$)
Surreal Spanish restaurant and tapas bar very popular with the Gen X crowd. Great ambience. Be prepared to wait.
➕ D2 ✉ 415 Washington Street (at Beacon Street), Somerville ☎ 661-3254 🕐 From 11:30 Ⓣ Harvard Square then walk

DAVIO'S ($$)
Enjoy reliable Northern Italian pastas in the formal downstairs dining room, or pizzas upstairs in a more casual setting.
➕ F5; G3 ✉ 269 Newbury Street; Hotel Sonesta, 5 Cambridge Pkwy, Cambridge ☎ 262-4810; 661 4810 🕐 Lunch, dinner Ⓣ Copley; Lechmere

MAMMA MARIA ($$$)
Very highly regarded North End Italian, offering imaginative cooking, elegant decor and gracious service with prices to match.
➕ dII/H4 ✉ 3 North Square ☎ 523-0077 🕐 Lunch Tue–Sat, dinner daily Ⓣ Haymarket

PIGNOLI ($/$$)
Inventive Italian-inspired cooking includes specialties such as Maine crab ravioli and Fishermen's zuppetta, an Italianate bouillabaisse. Huge paper lanterns are part of the eclectic decor. Serves late.
➕ G5 ✉ 91 Park Plaza ☎ 338-7500 Ⓣ Arlington

RISTORANTE TOSCANO ($$$)
One of the best, this is an elegant eatery with a genuine Italian ambience. Try the risotto. Excellent wine list.
➕ aIII/G4 ✉ 41–7 Charles Street ☎ 723-4090 🕐 Lunch, dinner Ⓣ Charles/MGH

UPSTAIRS AT THE PUDDING ($$$)
Northern Italy meets California in this romantic restaurant above Harvard's Hasty Pudding Club Theater.
➕ C3 ✉ 10 Holyoke Street, Cambridge ☎ 864-1933 🕐 Dinner daily, lunch Mon–Fri, brunch Sun Ⓣ Harvard Square

For vegetarians
If you do not eat fish, you may find you have a limited choice of main course in Boston. And although the salads are often interesting and good, on the whole restaurants rarely offer vegetable entrees. The Italian and Chinese restaurants are your best bet. In Harvard Square, try the Border Cafe (➤ 66). In Chinatown try Buddha's Delight, 5 Beach Street. And see also Chau Chow, Grendel's Den, and Jae's Café & Grill (➤ 67).

AMERICAN & MEXICAN

New England specialties

Try these: lobster, clam chowder, scrod, quahog (a large clam, pronounced "ko hog"), Boston baked beans (cooked long and slow in an earthenware pot), Boston cream pie (chocolate-covered and custard-filled), Indian pudding (cornmeal, milk and molasses cooked long and slow).

Suggestions for children

Particularly popular are: Bertucci's (S), a local chain serving pizza and pasta, ✉ 21 Brattle Street, Harvard Square, Cambridge ☎ 864-4748 and at Faneuil Hall ☎ 227-7889. Also in Harvard Square, Cybersmith ✉ 36 Church Street ☎ 492-5857, offers burgers and computer games. The cornucopia of foodstalls in Faneuil should suit everyone. The Hard Rock Café is a (loud) family favorite near Hancock Tower. ✉ 131 Clarendon Street ☎ 424-7625

AMERICAN

CAPITAL GRILLE ($$$)
A men's club atmosphere prevails at this throwback to pre-fat-counting days. Expect large steaks, good service, and a full-bodied wine list.
➕ F5 ✉ 359 Newbury Street ☎ 262-8900 ⏰ Dinner only ♿ Hynes/ICA

COTTONWOOD RESTAURANT AND CAFE ($$)
Creative southwestern food in lively surroundings —a favorite with margarita-sipping yuppies.
➕ G5; CI ✉ 222 Berkeley Street; Porter Exchange Mall, 1815 Mass Ave, Cambridge ☎ 247-2225; 661-7440 ⏰ Lunch, dinner ♿ Copley; Porter Square

HENRIETTA'S TABLE ($$)
This country kitchen-style restaurant—a favorite of cooking legend Julia Child—provides creative New England food matched with an all-American wine list.
➕ C3 ✉ Charles Hotel, 1 Bennett Street, Cambridge ☎ 661-5005 ⏰ Dinner, Sun brunch ♿ Harvard Square

HUNGRY I ($$$)
A tiny, intimate basement restaurant offering a small but inventive contemporary menu. Romantic.
➕ aIV/G4 ✉ 71 Charles Street ☎ 227-3524 ⏰ Lunch, dinner ♿ Charles Street

ICARUS ($$$)
A pleasant place for a quiet meal in an elegant setting. Excellent contemporary cooking, good wine list.
➕ G6 ✉ 3 Appleton Street ☎ 426-1790 ⏰ Dinner only, Sun brunch ♿ Back Bay

METROPOLIS CAFE ($)
A comfortable South End local with honest contemporary food, fairly well prepared; Saturday jazz brunch has superb chocolate chunk pancakes, Sunday brunch, too.
➕ G6 ✉ 584 Tremont Street ☎ 247-2931 ⏰ Lunch, dinner, brunch 8–3 Closed Mon ♿ Back Bay

MEXICAN

BORDER CAFE ($)
You may well have to wait in line at this frantic eatery popular with students. One of the best Tex Mex places in Cambridge.
➕ 2C ✉ 32 Church Street ☎ 864-6100 ⏰ Dinner only ♿ Harvard Square

CASA ROMERO ($$)
Romantic Back Bay Mexican serving rich dishes. In summer eat al fresco in the courtyard.
➕ F5 ✉ 30 Gloucester Street ☎ 536-4341 ⏰ Dinner only ♿ Hynes/ICA

MEXICAN CUISINE ($$)
The straightforward name is a clue to the success of this authentic favorite— seafood specialties are popular.
➕ C3 ✉ 1682 Mass Ave ⏰ Dinner only ♿ Harvard Square

ASIAN & MIDDLE EASTERN

BOMBAY CLUB ($$)
The buffet lunch is excellent value in this stylish Harvard Square Indian restaurant. Expect to pay more for dinner.
✚ C3 ✉ 57 JFK Street, Harvard Square, Cambridge ☎ 661-8100 ⊙ Lunch, dinner, Sun brunch ⊕ Harvard Square

CAFE SUSHI ($$)
Small, colorful Japanese restaurant with large choice of sushi, sashimi, and fish baked in foil.
✚ C3 ✉ 1105 Mass Ave, Cambridge ☎ 492-0434 ⊙ Lunch, dinner. Sun dinner only ⊕ Harvard Square

CHAU CHOW AND GRAND CHAU CHOW ($)
Chinatown favorites on opposite sides of the street. The former is pretty basic; Grand Chau Chow, serving Hong Kong style food, is classier. No reservations.
✚ H5 ✉ 52 and 41–5 Beach Street ☎ 426-6266; 292-5166 ⊕ Chinatown

GINZA ($$)
The in-place for Japanese food: superior sushi, maki, and tempura.
✚ H5 ✉ 14 Hudson Street ☎ 338-2261 ⊕ Chinatown

GRENDEL'S DEN ($)
The menu of this Bohemian eatery ranges from Middle Eastern to Indian, with cheese fondue, plenty of vegetarian options, and a serve-yourself salad bar.
✚ C3 ✉ 89 Winthrop Street, Harvard Square., Cambridge ☎ 491-1160 ⊙ Lunch, dinner ⊕ Harvard Square

GYUHAMA OF JAPAN ($$)
Sushi and loud rock music are the specialties at this Back Bay restaurant.
✚ F5 ✉ 27 Boylston Street ☎ 437-0188 ⊙ To 2AM ⊕ Copley

JAE'S CAFE & GRILL ($$)
The two branches provide a Pan-Asian menu, but sushi is the specialty. Both very busy.
✚ F6; E3 ✉ 520 Columbus Avenue; 1281 Cambridge Street, Inman Square, Cambridge ☎ 421-9405; 497-8380 ⊕ Prudential; Central Square

MARY CHUNG ($)
Splendid Chinese food in an unpromising Central Square location.
✚ D4 ✉ 464 Mass Ave, Cambridge ☎ 864-1991 ⊕ Central Square

PASTEUR RESTAURANT ($)
Two small Vietnamese eateries providing reliable beef noodle soups and other Vietnamese favorites.
✚ G5; H5 ✉ 682 Washington Street; 8 Kneeland Street ☎ 482-7467; 451-0247 ⊕ Chinatown

THAI VILLAGE ($$)
Authentic Thai cuisine—lemon grass shrimp soup, and mussel pancake—shines in this elegant South End restaurant.
✚ G6 ✉ 592 Tremont Street ☎ 536-6548 ⊙ Lunch, dinner. Sun dinner only ⊕ Back Bay

 Also ➤ 69 for Moon Villa.

Beer here!
Brewpubs are popping up all over Boston. In Back Bay, try Back Bay Brewing Company.
✚ H7 ✉ 755 Boylston Street ☎ 424-8300 ⊕ Copley
Also Samuel Adams Brewhouse.
✚ H7 ✉ 710 Boylston Street ☎ 536-2739 ⊕ Copley

BRUNCH, COFFEE, TEA & LATE EATING

Boston Bagels

If you want to see the full range of bagels, visit the Bruegger Bagel Bakery next to the Globe Corner Bookstore in School Street (open from 6:30AM), where the variations on a theme include plain, poppy, sesame, salt, garlic, onion, honey, grain, cinnamon, raisin, sundried tomato, pumpernickel, blueberry…

BRUNCH

Weekend brunch is entrenched. Check out:
► 62 for Aujourd'hui,
► 63 for Ritz Carlton,
► 66 for Henrietta's Table, Icarus; ► 67 for Bombay Club; ► 64 for Skipjacks, Turner Fisheries.

GARDNER MUSEUM CAFE ($)

Highly civilized weekend brunch, preferably before a (winter) afternoon concert. Also lunch (Mon–Fri).
✚ D6 ✉ 280 The Fenway ☎ 566-1088 ◷ 11–4 🚇 Museum

HOUSE OF BLUES ($$)

The Sunday Gospel Jazz Brunch at this Boston outpost of the L.A.-based chain is already an institution. Eat from the phenomenal buffet at one long, crowded table to stirring Southern jazz and blues. Book ahead.
✚ C3 ✉ 96 Winthrop Street, Cambridge ☎ 491-2583 ◷ Three seatings

COFFEE

Branches of Au Bon Pain ("ABP") and Starbucks all over town. Otherwise, try:

BISCOTTIS PASTICCERIA

Favorite North End bakery with a mouth-watering window display.
✚ dlll ✉ 95 Salem Street ☎ 227-8365 🚇 Haymarket

BLACKSMITH HOUSE

Al fresco coffee and good pastries in Harvard Square. Built 1811, this was home to Longfellow's "Village Blacksmith."
✚ C3 ✉ 56 Brattle Street, Cambridge ☎ 354-3036 🚇 Harvard Square

REBECCA'S BAKERY & COFFEE

Homemade everything to go, including buttery pastries, cake, and fresh fruit tarts.
✚ alll/G4 ✉ 70 Charles Street ☎ 742-9542 🚇 Charles

CAFFE PARADISO

Nice for an unhurried coffee or lunch in Harvard Square. Also in the North End (255 Hanover Street).
✚ C3 ✉ 1 Eliot Square ☎ 868-3240 🚇 Harvard Square

TO GO BAKERY

South End locals line up for the muffins, scones, and creamcheese cake.
✚ F7 ✉ 314 Shawmut Avenue ☎ 482-1015 ◷ From 6:30AM weekdays, 7 weekends 🚇 Back Bay

A SPECIAL TEA

THE BRISTOL (FOUR SEASONS HOTEL)

Traditional high tea is served daily 3–4:30 around the fire or overlooking the Public Garden. For details see under Late Eating.

COPLEY PLAZA

Worth it just for the decor, but an excellent tea is served as well.
✚ H8 ✉ Copley Square ☎ 267-5300 🚇 Copley

MUSEUM OF FINE ARTS

Tea and music in the

elegant Ladies' Committee Room.

⊞ E6 ✉ 465 Huntington Avenue ☎ 369-3487
🕐 Tue–Fri 2:30–4 Ⓜ Museum

RITZ LOUNGE

Put on your best behavior for dainty sandwiches, English teacake, mini fruit tarts—and, oh joy!, leaf tea. A harpist plays in the corner.

⊞ G5 ✉ Ritz Carlton Hotel, 15 Arlington Street ☎ 536-5700 Ⓜ Arlington

LATE EATING

In general, Bostonians eat early. For late eating, try Chinatown and some of the following:

BLUE DINER ($)

Play hits of the '40s and '50s on the jukebox in this old-fashioned Leather District diner.

⊞ H5 ✉ 150 Kneeland Street ☎ 338-4639 🕐 24 hours Fri–Sun, to 8/9PM Mon–Thu Ⓜ South Station

THE BRISTOL (FOUR SEASONS HOTEL) ($$)

Gorge on calorific desserts in the Viennese Dessert Buffet by the fire or overlooking Public Garden. Especially good for chocoholics. Also late dining.

⊞ G5 ✉ 200 Boylston Street ☎ 338-4400 🕐 Mon–Thu, Sun to 11.30PM. Fri–Sat to 12:30AM; Viennese Dessert Buffet Fri–Sat (also seasonal Thu) 9PM–midnight Ⓜ Arlington

CHEERS (BULL AND FINCH PUB) ($)

The place made famous by the perennially popular TV series. Bar food served until late (wait until the tourists have departed).

⊞ aIV/G5 ✉ 84 Beacon Street ☎ 227-9605 Ⓜ Arlington

MISTRAL ($$, $)

Eclectic French bistro menu and cheaper fare in the café.

⊞ F6 ✉ 221 Columbus Avenue ☎ 867-9300
🕐 11AM–1AM Ⓜ Back Bay

MOON VILLA ($)

The food's not special—mainstream Chinese fare—but a late-night visit here while the rest of Boston sleeps is an experience .

⊞ H5 ✉ 19 Edinboro Street ☎ 423-2061 🕐 To 4AM Ⓜ Chinatown

RED HAT CAFE ($)

Food till the small hours. Downstairs bar is full of students, upstairs is more sedate.

⊞ bIII/H4 ✉ 9 Bowdoin Street ☎ 523-2175 🕐 To 2AM Ⓜ Bowdoin

SONSIE ($$)

Hip Newbury Street haunt with eclectic cooking that ranges from French to Oriental. Windows fold back for on-street dining. Weekend brunch, morning bakery, lunch, bar, dinner till late.

⊞ F5 ✉ 327 Newbury Street ☎ 351-2500 🕐 7AM–1AM Ⓜ Hynes/ICA

Ice cream

There is some superb ice-cream to be had in Boston. Try:

Emack & Bolio's ice-cream, yogurt and juice bar (they claim to have invented the sublime cookies and cream ice-cream). ✉ 290 Newbury Street.

Billings & Stover Apothecary, an old time drugstore with a genuine soda fountain. ✉ Brattle Street, Harvard Square.

Steve's and Herrel's premium ice cream, both named after local ice cream wizard, Steve Herrel. Available in many stores.

JP Licks ✉ 280 Centre Street, Jamaica Plain.

Toscanini's ✉ Corner of Mass Ave and Main Street, Cambridge.

DISTRICTS & DEPARTMENT STORES

There are several clearly defined shopping areas in Boston, each with its own personality. If you have time for only one spree, choose Newbury Street, which has to be one of the most beautiful streets for shoppers in the country.

NEWBURY STREET

Running west from the Public Garden to Massachusetts Avenue through the Back Bay, Newbury Street's Victorian houses make a colorful corridor of enticing stores, galleries, and restaurants. Everything is here, from designer boutiques to secondhand clothes stores, from prestigious galleries to Tower Records, from names like Giorgio Armani to small independents, from sidewalk cafés to sophisticated restaurants. The east end of the street is the chic end, the west less so.
➕ F5 🚇 Arlington, Copley, Hynes

CHARLES STREET

This is another pleasant street of stores and restaurants, running north from the Public Garden through the flat area of Beacon Hill. It specializes in antiques stores but has one or two nice gift stores and galleries too, and a selection of places where you can eat a bite to eat.
➕ aIV/G4 🚇 Arlington, Charles

DOWNTOWN CROSSING

Street fashion and shoe stores, run of the mill jewelry stores, camera stores and the like, plus the city's main department stores—and the legendary bargain hunters' mecca, Filene's Basement (➤ 77). Encompassing part of Washington Street, Winter Street, and Bromfield Street, Downtown Crossing is mainly pedestrians-only.
➕ cIV/H5 🚇 Downtown Crossing

FANEUIL HALL MARKETPLACE

Souvenirs and New England crafts keep company with worthwhile fashion, accessories, pewter, household ware stores, a BosTix ticket agency booth (➤ 80), and plenty of eating options— all in and around three well-restored wharf buildings.
➕ aIII/H4 🚇 State

HARVARD SQUARE

Cambridge's Harvard Square is a maze of streets with dozens of bookstores (many stay open all evening), music stores and clothes stores—new and secondhand—much of it geared for the student population. It's an entertaining place too, with a wide variety of food and drink options. Check out Brattle Street, Church Street, Eliot Street (with the Charles Square complex just off), John F. Kennedy Street, and Dunster Street.
➕ C2/3 🚇 Harvard Square

PRUDENTIAL CENTER AND COPLEY PLACE

A vast undercover complex in Back Bay that

Art galleries

Newbury Street is the place to go if you are interested in buying paintings, prints, or sculpture. Many a pleasant hour can be spent browsing in the galleries here, stopping off in a café now and then. There's a concentration of them between Arlington and Exeter streets, displaying works by 18th- and 19th-century and contemporary artists.

encompasses two malls (see below), several hotels, and the Hynes Convention Center.

MALLS

CAMBRIDGESIDE GALLERIA

Scores of stores on three levels, some of which will appeal to the younger generation. Fashion outlets include Banana Republic, Guess?, J Crew, and Talbots. There are several footwear places (such as Nine West and Overland), music stores, a Disney store, pushcarts, eateries, branches of department stores Filene's and Sears.

✚ F3 ✉ 100 Cambridgeside Place 🕐 Mon–Sat 10–9:30; Sun 11–7 🚇 Lechmere or Kendall Square and free shuttle bus

CHESTNUT HILL

Mall at Chestnut Hill for stylish shopping in a classy suburb.

✚ Off A7 ✉ Hammond Pond Parkway, Chestnut Hill 🚇 Chestnut Hill and 15 minute walk

COPLEY PLACE

Copley is more refined than the Pru, to which it is connected by a covered bridge over Huntington Avenue. Elegant stores such as Tiffany's, Louis Vuitton, Gucci, and Nieman-Marcus jostle with outlets for trendy kitchenware, high-tech gadgets and very good crafts. There is a movie complex.

✚ F6 ✉ Huntington Avenue 🕐 Mon–Sat 10–7. Sun 12–6 🚇 Copley

PRUDENTIAL CENTER

A dozen clothes stores (including Ann Taylor, Chico's, Claiborne Men, Structures, and Original Levi's), some shoe and accessories stores, some specialty (e.g. stationery) and gift stores, and a hardware store. The Pru is also home to department stores Saks Fifth Avenue and Lord & Taylor, the Greater Boston Convention & Visitor Bureau, a post office, a food court and Legal Sea Foods.

✚ F5/6 ✉ Between Boylston Street and Huntington Avenue 🕐 Mon–Sat 10–8; Sun 11–6 🚇 Prudential

DEPARTMENT STORES

Boston's two major department stores face each other in Downtown Crossing: Macy's, the bigger (formerly Jordan Marsh), and Filene's. Underneath Filene's is Filene's Basement (➤ 77). Other stores have branches in malls (see above): In Harvard Square there is The Coop, which is the Harvard Cooperative Society, strong on books and posters. It was started as a non-profit store for students in 1882 and is now the biggest department store in the center of Cambridge.

CLOTHES & JEWELRY

Fashion from the British Isles

Next
Affordable, good-quality clothes and accessories for men, women, and children.

✉ 208 Newbury Street
☎ 236-6398

Laura Ashley
Feminine dresses, blouses, and knitwear for women and children.

✉ 83 Newbury Street
☎ 536-0505

Burberry's of London
Made their name with their plaid-lined raincoats. Full range of quality clothes for men and women.

✉ 2 Newbury Street
☎ 236-1000

Celtic Weavers
Chunky knitwear from Ireland in Aran wool and rich Celtic patterns.

✉ Faneuil Hall Marketplace

ALAN BILZERIAN
A fun one for window shopping (or buying, of course, if you're very rich or very outrageous) for little numbers from Jean-Paul Gaultier, Katharine Hamnett and the like.
➕ G5 ✉ 37 Newbury Street
☎ 536-1001 Ⓜ Arlington

BETSYS
Pretty things in natural fabrics and locally knitted sweaters.
➕ F5 ✉ 201 Newbury Street
☎ 536-1050 Ⓜ Copley

CASHMERE BOSTON
Tempting clothes for women and men, in a wide range of styles.
➕ F5 ✉ 114 Newbury Street
☎ 236-5700 Ⓜ Copley

CHARLES SUMNER
This women's clothes store is an institution, really.
➕ G5 ✉ 16 Newbury Street
☎ 536-6225 Ⓜ Arlington

CHICO'S
Comfortable, casual but stylish and affordable women's clothes, just that little bit different. Pants, vests, and tops in natural fibers.
➕ F6 ✉ Prudential Center
☎ 247-3771 Ⓜ Prudential

EILEEN FISHER
Natural fabrics in elegant, simple designs for women's smart, casual day and evening wear. Rich color range.
➕ J7 ✉ Copley Place
☎ 536-6800 Ⓜ Copley

EMPORIO ARMANI
Slightly less haute couture but more accessible price-wise than Giorgio Armani (also in Newbury Street, No. 22). Popular café (on the sidewalk in summer).
➕ G5 ✉ 210 Newbury Street
☎ 262-7300 Ⓜ Copley

HARLEY DAVIDSON
Leather jackets and all the authentic biker stuff. Also at 160 Newbury Street.
➕ F3 ✉ Cambridgeside Galleria ☎ 236-0840
Ⓜ Lechmere

JASMINE/SOLA/SOLA MEN
Chic young designer clothes and shoes in Harvard Square but that's way too pricey for the average student.
➕ C3 ✉ 37 Brattle Street
☎ 354-6043 Ⓜ Harvard Square

JOS A BANK
One of Newbury Street's stores for men's and women's clothes.
➕ F5 ✉ 122 Newbury Street
☎ 536-5050 Ⓜ Copley

JOSEPH ABBOUD
The stylishly rugged look in men's clothes. Also women's clothes. An attractive store.
➕ G5 ✉ 37 Newbury Street
☎ 266-4200 Ⓜ Arlington

LIMITED
This chain offers a full range of women's clothes from Chinos and chunky knitwear to suits and jackets. Normal designs to suit most ages and pockets.
➕ dIII/H4 ✉ Faneuil Hall Marketplace and in malls
Ⓜ State

LOUIS, BOSTON
High quality, expensive

clothing for men and women in a spacious store just off Newbury Street. Nice café.

➕ G5 ✉ 234 Berkeley Street ☎ 262-6100 🚇 Arlington

SERENDIPITY

Funky choice of ethnic designs from India, South America and Africa, plus jewelry. Also at 279 Newbury Street.

➕ C3 ✉ 1312 Mass Ave ☎ 661-7143 🚇 Harvard Square

SIMONS

Impeccable men's tailoring at this classic Proper Bostonian store in Copley Square. Alterations can be arranged on the premises.

➕ F5 ✉ 220 Clarendon Street ☎ 266-2345 🚇 Copley

TALBOTS

Classic women's clothes for work or leisure. Neat suits, shirts and pants, plus coats, casual wear, nightwear. Includes a full range of petite sizes. Also 25 School Street.

➕ F5 ✉ 500 Boylston Street ☎ 262-2981 🚇 Arlington, Copley

URBAN OUTFITTERS

Where the younger set comes to get that rugged look. Also funky household goods.

➕ C3 ✉ 11 JFK Street/Brattle Street ☎ 864-0070 🚇 Harvard Square

VICTORIA'S SECRET

The ultimate in silk, satin, and lace.

➕ dlll/H4 ✉ Faneuil Hall Marketplace and in malls ☎ 248-9761 🚇 State

SECONDHAND DESIGN

If you lust after a designer label but can't afford Newbury Street's boutiques, take a look at top quality "gently worn," i.e. secondhand clothes, often with designer labels, including:

CHIC REPEATS

Clothes for women and children.

➕ F5 ✉ 117 Newbury Street ☎ 536-8580 🚇 Copley

THE CLOSET

Fashion for men and women.

➕ F5 ✉ 175 Newbury Street ☎ 536-1919 🚇 Copley

DÉJÁ VU

For women only.

➕ F5 ✉ 222 Newbury Street ☎ 424-9020 🚇 Copley

JEWELRY

JOHN LEWIS INC

The jewelry displayed here is all designed and hand-crafted from solid metal and semiprecious stones in a local studio.

➕ F5 ✉ 97 Newbury Street ☎ 266-6665 🚇 Arlington

SHREVE, CRUMP & LOW

This is THE place to buy your diamonds, rubies, silver and gold. Aside from anything else, this is a landmark building of the art deco period and definitely worth a look inside.

➕ G5 ✉ 330 Boylston Street ☎ 267-9100 🚇 Arlington

Clothes for sports and the outdoor life

More casual clothes will be found in some of the stores listed under Shoes & Outdoor Gear (➤ 74).

SHOES & OUTDOOR GEAR

Renting bikes, rollerblades, skates

Back Bay Bicycles (bikes, skates)
🚇 G5 ✉ 333 Newbury Street
☎ 247-2336 Ⓜ Hynes
Bob Smith Sporting Goods
(rollerblades) see entry.

SHOES

ALLEN EDMONDS
Top quality shoes in classic styles come in sizes 5–18 and widths AAAA–EEEE.
🚇 G5 ✉ 36 Newbury Street
☎ 247-3363 Ⓜ Arlington

CHARLES SUMNER SHOE SALON
Chic women's shoes and handbags including Salvatore Ferragamo.
🚇 G5 ✉ 16 Newbury Street
☎ 536-0237 Ⓜ Arlington

FOOTPATHS
Elegant shoes for men and women, plus a full range of hiking boots.
🚇 H4 ✉ 489 Washington Street ☎ 338-6008
Ⓜ Downtown Crossing

OVERLAND TRADING
The wide selection of hiking shoes, boots and sneakers here includes Timberland, Sebago. Also in Cambridgeside Galleria.
🚇 F5 ✉ 176 Newbury Street
☎ 424-7615 Ⓜ Copley

THE ROCKPORT STORE
The main outlet here for Rockport shoes and boots.
🚇 dIII/H4 ✉ Faneuil Hall Marketplace ☎ 367-9996
Ⓜ State

SNYDER'S
Brandname shoes and boots, plus jeans, casual shirts, sweatshirts.
🚇 F5 ✉ 799 Boylston Street
☎ 536-2433 Ⓜ Copley

THE TANNERY
Wide range of hiking boots and sneakers (Vans, Timberland, Sebago, Rockport). Also in Brattle Street, Harvard Square.
🚇 F5 ✉ 402 Boylston Street
☎ 267-0899 Ⓜ Arlington

TIMBERLAND
The boot and shoe makers' own store.
🚇 G5 ✉ 71 Newbury Street
☎ 236-1368 Ⓜ Copley, Arlington

OUTDOOR GEAR

BOB SMITH SPORTING GOODS
All the latest for hiking, camping, tennis, swimming, fishing, and rollerblading. Also at 1048 Commonwealth Avenue.
🚇 dIV/H5 ✉ 9 Spring Lane (off Washington Street) ☎ 426-4440 Ⓜ State

BRITCHES GREAT OUTDOORS
Plaid shirts, jackets, and outdoor footwear for men.
🚇 F6 ✉ Prudential Center
Ⓜ Prudential

ST. MORITZ
Skis and clothes for all winter sports.
🚇 F5 ✉ 145 Newbury Street
☎ 236-1212 Ⓜ Copley

TENT CITY
Near North Station, good for hiking and camping.
🚇 cII/H4 ✉ 272 Friend City
☎ 227-9104 Ⓜ North Station

WAYLAND GOLF SHOP
The best names in clubs, bags, shoes, etc. Out beyond Boston University on T Green Line B.
🚇 Off map west ✉ 890 Commonwealth Avenue ☎ 894-2503 Ⓜ Green line B to Pleasant Street

BOOKS, MUSIC & MAPS

BOOKS, GUIDES & MAPS

AVENUE VICTOR HUGO
An institution. Huge collection of secondhand books on every subject.
📧 F5 ✉ 339 Newbury Street
☎ 266-7746/262-0880
🚇 Hynes

BRATTLE BOOKSTORE
A treasure trove of rare and secondhand books with a good section on Boston and New England.
📧 bIV/G5 ✉ 9 West Street
☎ 542-0210 🚇 Park

GLOBE CORNER BOOKSTORE
Great source for travel books and maps. (Also at 49 Palmer Street, Cambridge.) 📧 cIV/H4
✉ 500 Boylston Street ☎ 859-8008

GROLIER POETRY BOOKSHOP
One of the US's only stores devoted to poetry.
📧 6 Plympton Street, Cambridge.
☎ 547 4648

HARVARD BOOKSTORE
Venerable favorite for academic titles and non-fiction.
📧 1,256 Massachusetts Avenue, Cambridge. ☎ 661 1515

WATERSTONE'S
A retreat for book lovers in Faneuil. Another branch is at 26 Exeter/Newbury Street.
📧 dIII/H4 ✉ 30 Faneuil Hall Marketplace ☎ 589-0930
🚇 State

WORDSWORTH
An absolute warren. Discounted prices.
📧 C3 ✉ 30 Brattle Street
☎ 354-5201 🚇 Harvard Square

MUSIC

CHEAPO RECORDS
Used rock, blues, jazz albums, LPs and 45s.
📧 D4 ✉ 645 Mass Ave, Cambridge ☎ 354-4455
🚇 Central

HMV
A huge store covering all tastes in music.
📧 C3 ✉ 1 Brattle Street, Cambridge ☎ 868-9696
🚇 Harvard Square

NEWBURY COMICS
The hippest record store in town. Pop CDs plus T-shirts, posters and comics. Also in Cambridge at 36 JFK Street. and at the MIT Stratton Student Center, Mass Avenue.
📧 H5 ✉ 332 Newbury Street
☎ 236-4930 🚇 Hynes

TOWER RECORDS
The largest Tower store in the world. There's another in Cambridge at 95 Mt. Auburn Street.
📧 F5 ✉ 360 Newbury Street
☎ 247-5900 🚇 Hynes

ANTIQUE MAPS

EUGENE GALLERIES
A Beacon Hill store specializing in old maps and prints, with a good selection covering Boston and New England.
📧 aIV/G4 ✉ 76 Charles Street ☎ 227-3062
🚇 Charles

Shopping with/for children

In Harvard Square:

Curious George goes to WordsWorth
WordsWorth's children's book store, full of delights.
📧 C3 ✉ Brattle Street
☎ 498-0062 🚇 Harvard Square
Learningsmith
Superb choice of books, games and educational toys for children of all ages.
📧 C3 ✉ 25 Brattle Street
☎ 661-6008 🚇 Harvard Square

In Faneuil Hall Marketplace:

Kites of Boston and the **New England Cloth Doll Co** are good bets.

In Back Bay there is the toy emporium **FAO Schwarz**
📧 F5 ✉ 440 Boylston Street
☎ 262-5900 🚇 Arlington

Museums with particularly good stores for children are:
the Children's Museum (➤ 59),
the Computer Museum (➤ 47),
the Museum of Fine Arts (➤ 28),
the Museum of Science (➤ 34).

ANTIQUES, CRAFTS & GIFTS

Food

For New England specialties, wine, beers, and gourmet foods try Cardullo's in Harvard Square.

➕ C3 ✉ 6 Brattle Street
☎ 491-8888 🚇 Harvard Square

For anything and everything Italian in the food line, explore the stores in the North End.

For fruit and vegetables there's Boston's only street market, Blackstone Market, on Fridays and Saturdays near Faneuil Hall Marketplace.

➕ F14 ✉ Blackstone Street
🚇 Haymarket, State

ANTIQUES

BOSTON ANTIQUE CENTER

A warehouseful of top-price antique furniture, rugs and artifacts, with one floor devoted to British dealers.

➕ cII/H4 ✉ 54 Canal Street
🕐 Closed Mon ☎ 742-1400
🚇 Haymarket

CAMBRIDGE ANTIQUE MARKET

150 dealers, selling china, glass, quilts, clothes, silver, jewelry and collectibles, just across the river. Café.

➕ F3 ✉ 201 Monsignor O'Brien Highway 🕐 Closed Mon ☎ 868-9655
🚇 Lechmere

CHARLES STREET

This pretty street at the foot of Beacon Hill is lined with a string of 30 or so antique stores, mostly fairly pricey. They're in basements, on second floors and down alleys, and there are a few more in River Street. Between them they sell everything from 18th- and 19th-century European furniture to porcelain and lighting, linens and garden furnishings.

➕ aIII–IV/G4 🚇 Arlington, Charles

BROMFIELD PEN SHOP

Vintage pens from the early 1900s plus new ones from Montblanc, Cross, and other market leaders.

➕ cIV/H5 ✉ 5 Bromfield Street ☎ 482-9053 🚇 Park

NOSTALGIA FACTORY

Thousands of original film posters (some vintage), old signs, advertisements, etc.

➕ F5 ✉ 336 Newbury Street
☎ 236-8754 🚇 Hynes

For antique maps ➤ 75.

CRAFTS & GIFTS

For art see panel (➤ 70)

BROOKSTONE

Hundreds of nifty little gadgets.

➕ F6 ✉ Copley Place
☎ 267-4308 🚇 Copley

CAMBRIDGE ARTISTS' COOPERATIVE

Quilts, weaving, jewelry, scarves, bowls—all made locally and mostly affordable.

➕ C3 ✉ 59A Church Street
☎ 868-4434 🚇 Harvard

J OLIVER'S

Crammed with tasteful and fun gifts.

➕ aIV/G4 ✉ 38 Charles Street ☎ 227-4646
🚇 Arlington

SIGNATURE

Top American crafts. On the fringe of Faneuil.

➕ F14 ✉ 24 North Street
☎ 227-4885 🚇 State

SOCIETY OF ARTS AND CRAFTS

Superb contemporary ceramics, glass, woodwork and jewelry of the highest quality.

➕ F5 ✉ 175 Newbury Street
☎ 266-1810 🚇 Copley

DISCOUNT SHOPPING

FILENE'S BASEMENT

Centrally located, this is a Boston institution, the original bargain basement, beneath Filene's department store but now separately managed. When a store or manufacturer has overstock (or goes under) the goods end up here and are sold off at vastly discounted prices. The price is then marked down again and again over a period of several weeks until sold. As you can imagine, the Basement gets incredibly crowded, so avoid lunchtime and the weekend.

✚ clV/H5 ✉ Washington Street at Summer Street ☎ 542-2011 Ⓔ Downtown crossing

OUTLET SHOPPING

Factory outlet shopping is now one of New England's biggest draws for visitors. The major outlet centers are all out of Boston, not much more than an hour, so once you're there, especially if you are staying a few days, you may well find the trip irresistible. A whole range of merchandise—clothes, shoes, household and electrical goods, luggage—is discounted, sometimes as much as 70 percent off the normal retail price. All the well-known brand names keep cropping up, including Levi's, Calvin Klein, Liz Claiborne, Van Heusen, Ralph Lauren, Timberland, Bally, and Eddie Bauer.

Closest to Boston are:

KITTERY, Maine (about an hour north on Route 95) where there are over 100 stores. Here the Kittery Trading Post is a major draw for outdoor clothes and equipment. Other big names include Levi's, Liz Claiborne, Calvin Klein, Donna Karan.

FREEPORT, Maine, north of Kittery, is the birthplace of outlet shopping, where outdoor clothing specialist L. L. Bean features along with Ralph Lauren, Laura Ashley, Dexter Shoes, Dansk, and many more.

WORCESTER COMMON About one hour west on Route 1/90 or by Peter Pan bus from South Station, this outlet has dozens of men's, women's and children's clothes and shoe stores, including Esprit, Bally, Benetton, Levi's, Polo Ralph Lauren, Van Heusen.

FALL RIVER One hour south of Boston, Fall River is particularly known for linens, kitchenware, and furniture.

Farther afield, the outlets in New Hampshire are especially popular because there is no state sales tax. Mecca is North Conway, with just about every brand name under the sun.

The savvy outlet shopper

Check carefully for damage or flaws. Be aware that some stores sell at normal retail prices as well as discount prices. The best times to shop in outlets is in the summer for winter clothes, in the winter for summer clothes. Another good time is after Christmas, when stores are having a clear out to make way for the new season's stock.

Check the refund policy. Some stores give a refund, some only credit or exchange.

CLASSICAL MUSIC, OPERA & DANCE

Star of the classical music scene is the Boston Symphony Orchestra, which performs regularly from October to April. Keep an eye out for the many high-caliber performances that are free.

CONCERT HALLS

BERKLEE PERFORMANCE CENTER

This revamped building in Back Bay seats 1,220 and hosts a series of varied concerts by international performers and by the students and staff of the Berklee College of Music.
✚ E6 ✉ 136 Massachusetts Avenue ☎ 266-7455/266-1400 ext 261 Ⓒ Hynes Convention Center

BOSTON UNIVERSITY CONCERT HALL

Students show off their musical talents, in free public concerts.
✚ D5 ✉ Tsai Performance Center, 685 Commonwealth Avenue ☎ 353-6467 Ⓒ Boston University Central

HATCH MEMORIAL SHELL

Boston Pops Orchestra gives free evening concerts at this site on the Charles River Esplanade in July. Highlight is the 4th of July concert, with fireworks. Bring a blanket and a picnic.
✚ G4 ✉ Esplanade, Embankment Road ☎ 523-8881 Ⓒ Charles, Arlington

JORDAN HALL

Restored to its glittering glory in 1995, this acoustically perfect venue in the prestigious New England Conservatory showcases the resident Boston Philharmonic, Boston Baroque, Cantata Singers, and Boston Gay Men's Chorus. Conservatory students perform hundreds of free concerts throughout the year.
✚ F6 ✉ 30 Gainsborough Street ☎ 262-1120/536-2412 Ⓒ Symphony

SANDERS THEATRE

A 1,200-seat neo-gothic theater at Harvard, with a varied program of classical music and other fare.
✚ C2 ✉ Cambridge/Quincy streets, Cambridge ☎ 496-2420 Ⓒ Harvard Square

SYMPHONY HALL

Home of the world-renowned Boston Symphony Orchestra for seven months of the year. From October to April the orchestra performs on Friday afternoons and Saturday, Tuesday, and Thursday evenings, and open rehearsals are held some Wednesday evenings and Thursday mornings. The Boston Pops Orchestra concerts (started in 1885 and still as popular as ever) are held here in May and June before moving to the Hatch Memorial Shell in July.
✚ F6 ✉ 301 Massachusetts Avenue ☎ 266-1492/266-2378 Ⓒ Symphony

SMALLER VENUES & CHAMBER MUSIC

EMMANUEL CHURCH

A Bach cantata is

Choral and early music groups

Boston has more than its fair share of choirs and early music groups, including the oldest music organization in the U.S.: the Handel & Haydn Society, established in 1815 and still performing regularly (at Symphony Hall). Other groups to look for are Boston Camerata, for medieval music ☎ 262-2092; Chorus Pro Musica, for classical choral work and opera ☎ 267-7442; and the Cantata Singers, based at Jordan Hall, for Bach to contemporary works ☎ 267-6502.

performed every Sunday (Sep–May).

✚ G9 ✉ 15 Newbury Street
☎ 536-3355 🚇 Arlington

ISABELLA STEWART GARDNER MUSEUM

The great turn-of-the-century patron of arts and music began hosting chamber concerts in the Tapestry Room of her Venetian-style mansion (▶ 27), and the museum still runs concerts here on weekend afternoons (Sep–Apr).

✚ G5 ✉ 280 The Fenway
☎ 566-1401 🚇 Museum

KING'S CHAPEL

Free lunchtime concerts every Tuesday (12:15); vocal and organ recitals.

✚ D6 ✉ 58 Tremont Street
☎ 523-1749 🚇 State/Government Center

MUSEUM OF FINE ARTS

Baroque chamber concerts by the Boston Museum Trio and others given in the Remis Auditorium on Sunday afternoons September to May, jazz concerts in the courtyard onWednesday evenings in summer (▶ 28).

✚ E6 ✉ 465 Huntington Avenue ☎ 267-9300
🚇 Museum

TRINITY CHURCH

The rich interior of this architectural landmark (▶ 32) makes a wonderful backdrop for free organ and choir recitals, Friday lunchtimes (12:15).

✚ F5 ✉ Copley Square
☎ 536-0944 🚇 Copley

OPERA & DANCE

BOSTON LYRIC OPERA COMPANY

A fast-growing opera company (☎ 542-6772) that performs three productions a season at the Emerson Majestic Theater (below).

✚ G5 ✉ 114 State Street
☎ 248-8810 🚇 Downtown

DANCE UMBRELLA

The exciting Cambridge dance company draws on every imaginable movement vocabulary including that of the street.

✚ D4 ✉ 380 Green Street, Cambridge ☎ 492-7578
🚇 Central

EMERSON MAJESTIC THEATER

Innovative works performed by the Ballet Theater of Boston (☎ 262-0961), and by visiting troupes who explore other dance forms, such as flamenco.

✚ G5 ✉ 219 Tremont Street
☎ 578-8727 🚇 Boylston

THE WANG CENTER FOR THE PERFORMING ARTS

This movie palace dating from the 1920s is now used for concerts, opera, and dance, and is the home of the impressive Boston Ballet (☎ 695-6950), which performs classical and modern dance.

✚ G5 ✉ 268 Tremont Street
☎ 482-9393 🚇 Boylston

Alternative dance

Contemporary and ethnic dance troupes perform at venues all over the city and beyond. In Boston, these include the Dance Collective ☎ 576-2737; Beth Soll & Co ☎ 547-8771; and Art of Black Dance and Music ☎ 666-1859. In Cambridge, look for the Multicultural Arts Center ✉ 41 2nd Street ☎ 577-1400 and, in spring, a series of performances and workshops is held every year by the 30-member Mandala Folk Dance Ensemble ☎ 445-7515.

THEATER & MOVIES

Boston, once regarded as something of a theatrical backwater, has now a proliferation of fringe, student, and innovative companies, adding spice to the worthy mainstream fare. The city also benefits from a wide choice of movie theaters showing alternative films.

Tickets

BosTix sell half-price theater tickets on the day of the show (from 11AM). As a full-fledged Ticket Master outlet, it also sells full-price tickets in advance for venues in Boston and the rest of New England. Booths are at Faneuil Hall Marketplace (Tue–Sat 10–6; Sun 11–4) and Copley Square (Mon–Sat 10–6; Sun 11–4) and tickets cover theater, concerts, museums, sports events, and trolley tours. All are sold for cash only.

THEATER

AMERICAN REPERTORY THEATER

An award-winning professional repertory company based in Harvard Square and staging a wide range of classical and original drama.
➕ C4 ✉ Loeb Drama Center, 64 Brattle Street, Cambridge ☎ 547-8300 Ⓣ Harvard Square

BOSTON CENTER FOR THE ARTS

Four stages provide the space for several contemporary theater companies, including the resident Coyote Theater, bringing new life to Boston's theatrical scene.
➕ G6 ✉ 539 Tremont Street ☎ 426-7700 Ⓣ Back Bay

CHARLES PLAYHOUSE

Shear Madness is a comedy whodunnit set in a hairdresser's, which has played here since 1980.
➕ G5 ✉ 74 Warrenton Street ☎ 426-6912 Ⓣ Boylston

COLONIAL THEATER

This lush, beautifully restored, turn-of-the-century theater stages pre-Broadway productions as well as concerts and other performing arts events.
➕ G5 ✉ 106 Boylston Street ☎ 426-9366 Ⓣ Boylston

EMERSON MAJESTIC THEATER (➤ 79)

HASTY PUDDING THEATER

Home to the touring Harvard's Hasty Pudding company and to the Cambridge Theater Co., which stages new and unconventional productions.
➕ C3 ✉ 12 Holyoke Street, Cambridge ☎ 496-8400 Ⓣ Harvard Square

HUNTINGTON THEATER COMPANY

The varied program from Boston University's resident professional troupe includes European and American, classical and modern, comedies, and musicals.
➕ F6 ✉ 264 Huntington Avenue ☎ 266-0800 Ⓣ Symphony

LYRIC STAGE

Classics and new American shows are the specialty of this venue on the second floor of the YWCA building.
➕ F5 ✉ 140 Clarendon Street ☎ 437-7172 Ⓣ Back Bay

PUPPET SHOWPLACE THEATER

The trip out to suburban Brookline is well worth while for children—and adults—who enjoy puppetry.
➕ C7 ✉ 32–3 Station Street, Brookline ☎ 731-6400 Ⓒ Shows Sat, Sun 1 & 3; summer vacation daily 11 & 1; other school holidays daily 1 & 3

🔘 Brookline Village (Green Line D)

SHUBERT THEATER

An institution, founded in 1910, in the heart of the Theater District, which produces major pre- and post-Broadway shows.

➕ G5 ✉ 265 Tremont Street ☎ 426-4520 🔘 Boylston

STAGE ONE PLAYHOUSE

Light entertainment from karaoke to nostalgia. Dinner included.

➕ G5 ✉ 100 Warrenton Street ☎ 426-0300 🔘 Boylston

WILBUR THEATER

A small theater offering both new and classic drama.

➕ G5 ✉ 246 Tremont Street ☎ 451-2345 🔘 Boylston

MOVIES

BOSTON PUBLIC LIBRARY

The occasional film series usually features lesser-known old movies.

➕ F5 ✉ Copley Square ☎ 536-5400 🔘 Copley

BRATTLE THEATER

Old movies and film festivals attract connoisseurs to this small one-screen cinema.

➕ C3 ✉ 40 Brattle Street, Cambridge ☎ 876-6837 🔘 Harvard Square

COOLIDGE CORNER THEATER

A fine art deco Brookline venue showing an interesting and intelligent selection of vintage and contemporary films.

➕ C6 ✉ 290 Harvard Street, Brookline ☎ 734-2501 🔘 Coolidge Corner Green Line C Branch

HARVARD FILM ARCHIVE

Several daily showings of cult and independent movies at Harvard's Carpenter Center for the Visual Arts.

➕ C3 ✉ 24 Quincy Street, Cambridge ☎ 495-4700 🔘 Harvard Square

LANDMARK'S KENDALL SQUARE CINEMA

A multi-screen cinema also showing offbeat and foreign films.

➕ F4 ✉ 1 Kendall Square, Cambridge ☎ 494-9800 🔘 Broadway

MUSEUM OF FINE ARTS

Early movies, local interest and other offbeat films at the museum's Remis Auditorium (▶ 28)

➕ E6 ✉ 465 Huntington Avenue ☎ 267-9300 🔘 Museum

SONY NICKELODEON

Often shows foreign and independent films. The centrally located Sony commercial multiplex shows first runs.

➕ D5 ✉ 606 Commonwealth Avenue ☎ 424-1500 🔘 Kenmore/ Boston University East

A bit of variety

Fans of old-time vaudeville might like to take a trip out of Boston to Beverly, where Le Grand David and His Own Spectacular Magic Company offer good old-fashioned entertainment at the Cabot Street Cinema Theater ✉ 286 Cabot Street every Sun and on some Sats and holidays at the Larcom Theater ✉ 13 Wallis Street ☎ 508 927 3677

Clubs & Bars

Waterfront concerts

In summer pop concerts are held in the white Harborlights tent on Fan Pier, Northern Avenue. Tickets are expensive, but with the views of the downtown skyline, you may not mind.

☎ 737-6100/443-0161
🚇 South Station

Quieter choices

If you'd rather hear yourself think than groove the night away, check out Boston hotels' lounge bars—many with low-key music, some with food. Try Copley's, the elegant bar at the Copley Plaza Hotel, Copley Square (➤ 84); Turner Fisheries Bar at Westin Hotel, Huntington Avenue, where a pianist plays Sunday through Wednesday and a trio Thursday through Saturday; the Bristol Lounge in the Four Seasons Hotel (➤ 69), where classical piano or jazz music accompanies the sublime Viennese Dessert Buffet; the Atrium Lounge at the Regal Bostonian Hotel, Faneuil Hall, where a jazz pianist plays Monday through Friday, 5–7. See also the Regattabar and Scullers entries.

JAZZ & BLUES

HOUSE OF BLUES
A well-equipped venue featuring live music and a very popular Sunday gospel group brunch.
➕ C3 ✉ 96 Winthrop Street, Cambridge ☎ 491-2583
🕐 Live shows from 10PM; brunch 3 sittings 🚇 Harvard Square

JOHNNY D'S
Good food and fine sounds in Somerville's Davis Square, just north of Cambridge.
➕ Off map 1B ✉ 17 Holland Street, Somerville ☎ 778-2004
🚇 Davis Square

REGATTABAR
First-class jazz acts in a pleasant bar in the Charles Hotel, with an annual festival January through April.
➕ C3 ✉ 1 Bennett Street, Cambridge ☎ 864-1200/876-7777 🕐 Closed Sun, Mon
🚇 Harvard Square

RYLES
Another Cambridge hot-spot, in Inman Square, offering serious jazz, with food downstairs.
➕ D3 ✉ 212 Hampshire Street, Cambridge ☎ 876-9330
🕐 7PM–1AM (Sun brunch 10–4)
🚇 Central and walk

SCULLERS
Famous names perform great jazz at this bar in the Doubletree Suites Hotel, Tuesday to Saturday. Reserve in advance.
➕ C4 ✉ 400 Soldiers Field Road at River Street Bridge
☎ 783-0811

STICKY MIKE'S
A blues bar in the Theater District that's friendly, intimate and comfortable.
➕ G5 ✉ 5 Boylston Place
☎ 262-2605 🚇 Boylston

WALLY'S CAFE
Local jazz musicians play to a loyal audience, some of whom attend the New England Conservatory of Music nearby.
➕ J5 ✉ 427 Mass Ave
☎ 424-1408
🚇 Symphony/Mass Ave

WILLOW JAZZ CLUB
Music for dedicated jazz-lovers in atmospheric, smoky surroundings near Tufts University campus in Somerville.
➕ Off map A1 ✉ 699 Broadway, Ball Square ☎ 623-9874

MUSIC & DANCE CLUBS

AVALON
Combining live acts and dance, Avalon offers a good mix: international music Thursday and Friday, mainstream on Saturday and house on Sunday.
➕ E5 ✉ 15 Lansdowne Street
☎ 262-2424 🕐 10PM–2PM
🚇 Kenmore

AXIS
Next door to Avalon, and sharing a combined admission night with it on Sunday (gay night). House and Jungle on Tuesday, live bands on Wednesday, '70s soul music on Thursday, and house on Friday, with house at weekends.
➕ E5 ✉ 7 Lansdowne Street
☎ 262-2437 🕐 10:30PM–2AM
🚇 Kenmore

M-80

Trendspot for chic ravers. The powerful sound system can be deafening, so have your conversation before entering.

✚ D5 ✉ 696 Commonwealth Avenue ☎ 351-2527 Ⓜ Kenmore

VENUS DE MILO

Another Lansdowne Street favorite, offering DJ and live music in a neo-gothic ballroom. Joins forces with nearby Bill's Bar on Tuesday for live rock and Thursday for dance.

✚ E5 ✉ 11 Lansdowne Street ☎ 421-9595 Ⓒ Tue–Sat 10PM–2AM Ⓜ Kenmore

ZANZIBAR

Tropical décor, complete with 20-ft. palm trees. The music covers techno on Tuesday, '70s on Wednesday, alternative on Thursday, and top-100 hits on weekends.

✚ G5 ✉ 1 Boylston Place ☎ 451-1955 Ⓒ Wed 9PM–2AM; Thu–Sat 10PM–2AM Ⓜ Boylston

BARS, COMEDY & GAMES

BOSTON BILLIARD CLUB

Popular Fenway Park hangout for pool addicts.

✚ D6 ✉ 126 Brookline Avenue ☎ 536-POOL Ⓜ Kenmore

BULL & FINCH

The original *Cheers* pub, carried here from the U.K. and rebuilt before inspiring the TV sitcom. You'll know it by the lines of tourists outside.

✚ aIV/G5 ✉ 84 Beacon Street ☎ 227-9605 Ⓜ Arlington

COMEDY CONNECTION

A top-rate comedy club with shows every night, two on Friday, and three on Saturday. Reservations are a good idea.

✚ dIII/H4 ✉ Faneuil Hall Marketplace ☎ 248-9700 Ⓒ Shows Sun–Thu 8:30PM; Fri 8:30 & 10:30PM; Sat 7, 9 & 11PM Ⓜ State

DICK DOHERTY'S COMEDY VAULT

One of the leading comedy clubs, set in a former bank vault; shows Thursday to Saturday.

✚ G5 ✉ 124 Boylston Street ☎ 267-6626 Ⓜ Boylston

JILLIAN'S

An essential stop for virtual reality and pool fans, with over 200 high-tech games, virtual sports and 50 pool tables, not to mention the five bars and bistro-style food.

✚ E6 ✉ 145 Ipswich Street ☎ 437-0300 Ⓒ Pool Hall: Mon–Sat 11AM–2AM, Sun 12PM–2AM. Games: Mon–Fri 5PM–2AM; Sat 11AM–2AM; Sun 12PM–2AM Ⓜ Kenmore

NICK'S COMEDY STOP

A well-loved theater district comedy club with local stars and would-be stars on stage.

✚ G5 ✉ 100 Warrenton Street ☎ 482-0930 Ⓒ Shows Sun–Thu 8:30PM, Fri 8:30 & 10:30PM, Sat 8, 10 & 11:30PM Ⓜ Boylston

Nightlife and harbor cruises

Odyssey operates moonlight cruises (Fri and Sat 10:30PM) on a 600-passenger yacht, as well as Sunday dinner cruises (5–9PM), a Sunday jazz brunch and weekday lunches (11:15–2:15), sailing from Rowes Wharf ✉ Atlantic Avenue ☎ 946-7245.

The Spirit of Boston has live bands and shows on its dinner dance cruises, and sails from 60 Rowes Wharf (behind the Boston Harbor Hotel). Dinner cruises Mon–Thu 6:30–10; Fri and Sat 8–11:30; Sun 5:30–9; lunch cruises, also with music, daily 11–2 (from 11:30 Mon–Sat out of season) ☎ 457-1450

LUXURY HOTELS

Special deals

You may pay over $250 per night for a double room in the hotels on this page. On the other hand, with prices varying according to days of the week and the time of year, some hotel rates lie in the Mid-Range category. Always ask if there are any special deals. If you have children, ask about family packages. Some hotels also offer theater weekends.

Health and fitness

Unless otherwise noted, all hotels listed on this page and on page 85 either have fitness centers and pools within the hotel or offer complimentary use of nearby health spas.

Green hotels

Hotels such as the Lenox and Copley Square have introduced programs that encourage staff and guests to save water and energy. For instance, guests may opt to re-use linens for a second night.

BOSTON HARBOR

Modern, elegant and right on the waterfront, where cruiseboats and the airport shuttle ferry dock. It's worth paying a little more for a room with harbor views. Top restaurant, with views to match.
⊞ clV/H4 ✉ 7 Rowes Wharf
☎ 439-7000 or 800 752-7077; fax 330 9450 🚇 Aquarium

BOSTON PARK PLAZA & TOWERS

Elegant hotel built in 1927. Near Public Garden and Theater District. Business facilities. Family friendly.
⊞ G5 ✉ 64 Arlington Street
☎ 426-2000 or (800) 225-2008; fax 426-5545
🚇 Arlington

BOSTONIAN

More intimate than some, the Bostonian offers comfort without glitz. Seasons Restaurant. Right by Faneuil Hall.
⊞ dlV/H4 ✉ Faneuil Hall Marketplace ☎ 523-3600 or 800 343-0922; fax 523-2454
🚇 State, Government Center

COPLEY PLAZA

A "grand dame" of Boston, famed for its sumptuous decor (if you don't stay here, do at least take a tour). In Copley Square.
⊞ F5 ✉ 138 St. James Avenue ☎ 267-5300 or 800 822-4200; fax 267-7668
🚇 Copley

FOUR SEASONS

Everything you could ask for in elegance and personal attention. Home of Aujourd'hui and Bristol restaurants, overlooking the Public Garden.
⊞ G5 ✉ 200 Boylston Street
☎ 338-4400 or 800 332-3442; fax 426-7199 🚇 Arlington

LE MERIDIEN

In a historic 1920s building in the heart of the Financial District. Julien restaurant, business center.
⊞ dlV/H4 ✉ 250 Franklin Street (Post Office Square)
☎ 451-1900 or 800 543-4300; fax 423-2844 🚇 State, Downtown Crossing

OMNI PARKER

A rather staid 19th-century establishment, a block from the Common. Chefs from this hotel invented two of the mainstays of traditional American cooking—the Parker House roll and Boston cream pie.
⊞ clV/H6 ✉ 60 School Street
☎ 227-8600 or (800) 843-6664; fax 742-5729 🚇 Park

RITZ-CARLTON

The ultimate in graciousness and elegance. Stop in the lounge for tea, the bar for martinis, the dining room for dinner, or the café for after-theater. Overlooks Newbury Street and the Public Garden.
⊞ G5 ✉ 15 Arlington Street
☎ 536-5700 or 800 241-3333; fax 536-1335 🚇 Arlington

WESTIN

Handsome rooms in a 36-story hotel with direct access to Copley Place mall. Jazz nightly in the Turner Fisheries Bar.
⊞ F5 ✉ 10 Huntington Avenue ☎ 262-9600 or 800 228-3000; fax 424-7483
🚇 Copley

MID-RANGE HOTELS

BACK BAY HILTON
Standard Hilton comfort, plus business services—photocopying and fax facilities. Convenient to the Pru and Hynes Convention Center.

➕ F6 ✉ 40 Dalton Street ☎ 236-1100 or 800-HILTONS; fax 236-1506 🚇 Prudential/Hynes Convention Center

COLONNADE
A small independent hotel, near the Prudential Center and Symphony Hall.

➕ F6 ✉ 120 Huntington Avenue ☎ 424-7000 or 800 962-3030; fax 424-1717 🚇 Prudential

COPLEY SQUARE
Turn-of-the-century hotel with European flavor. Follows a green policy. For Café Budapest (▶ 62). No fitness center or pool.

➕ F5 ✉ 47 Huntington Avenue ☎ 536-9000 or 800 225-7062; fax 267-3547 🚇 Copley

ELIOT
Elegance, comfort and good value (though not the best location on Commonwealth Avenue). The hotel is all suites, each with a living room and kitchenette.

➕ F5 ✉ 370 Commonwealth Avenue ☎ 267-1607 or 800 44 ELIOT; fax 536-9114 🚇 Hynes Convention Center

LENOX
Built 1900 and beautifully renovated with period details, this independent is one of the best. Adopts a green policy. In-room fax.

➕ F5 ✉ 710 Boylston Street

☎ 536-5300 or 800 225-7676; fax 266-7905 🚇 Copley

MARRIOTT COPLEY PLACE
38-floor hotel in the heart of Copley Place shopping center. Covered walkway to Pru/Hynes.

➕ F6 ✉ 110 Huntington Avenue ☎ 236-5800 or 800 228-9290 fax 424-9378 🚇 Prudential, Copley

MARRIOTT LONG WHARF
Built like an ocean liner, this hotel has a fine harborside position. Business center. Close to Faneuil.

➕ clll/J4 ✉ 296 State Street (Long Wharf) ☎ 227-0800 or 800 228-9290; fax 227-2867 🚇 Aquarium

SHERATON & SHERATON TOWERS
A large one, in the Pru/Hynes. The Towers is more luxurious, butlers available on request.

➕ F6 ✉ Prudential Center, 39 Dalton Street ☎ 236-2000 or 800 325-3535; fax 236-6061 🚇 Prudential

SWISSÔTEL
The plain, modern façade belies classic European elegance inside. Exemplary service and a downtown location make it a good choice for business or sightseeing.

➕ cV/H5 ✉ 1 Avenue de Lafayette ☎ 451-2600 or 800 621-9200; fax 451-0054 🚇 Downtown Crossing

Prices
Expect to pay $150–250 for a double room in the hotels on this page, but see panel opposite.

Staying in Cambridge
Options include:

The **Hyatt Regency**, on the Charles, which has a revolving rooftop lounge ➕ D5 ✉ 575 Memorial Drive ☎ 492-1234 or 800 233-1234; fax 491-6906

A **Cambridge House**, an old bed-and-breakfast inn, furnished with antiques, in north Cambridge ➕ C1 ✉ 2218 Mass Avenue ☎ 491-6300 or 800 232-9989; fax 868 2848 🚇 Porter Square

Airport hotels
Harborside Hyatt Luxury conference center and hotel ☎ 568-1234 or 800 233-1234; fax 567-8856 🚇 Airport

Hilton Mid-price range ☎ 569-9300 or 800 722-5004; fax 569-3981 🚇 Airport

Holiday Inn Cheaper price range ☎ 569-5250 or 800 465-4329; fax 569-5159 🚇 Airport

BUDGET ACCOMMODATIONS

Prices

You should get a double room in the hotels listed here for under $100.

B&B accommodations range from $70 to $140, double occupancy

Out of town

When every hotel room in Boston seems to be taken up with conventioneers—as is often the case—consider staying in towns such as Quincy, Concord, or Salem, all charming places only 30–40 minutes from Boston. Each has a choice of places to stay and eat and there are regular train services.

Contact DestINNations for help with reservations ✉ PO Box 1173, Osterville MA 02655 ☎ 508 790-0577; fax 508 790-0565.

BEST WESTERN BOSTON

Out near medical complexes and Fenway Park.
✚ D7 ✉ 342 Longwood Avenue ☎ 731 4700 or 800 528 1234; fax 731-4850 🚇 Longwood

CHANDLER INN

Cheap basic hotel in the attractive South End district. Not far from Copley/Pru.
✚ G6 ✉ 26 Chandler Street ☎ 482-3450 or 800 842-3540; fax 542-3428 🚇 Back Bay

HOLIDAY INN

A functional base at the foot of Beacon Hill's north slope.
✚ G4 ✉ 5 Blossom Street ☎ 742-7630 or 800 HOLIDAY; fax 742-4192 🚇 Charles, Bowdoin

HOWARD JOHNSON LODGE FENWAY

Next door to Fenway Park, convenient to Red Sox games. Also near major art galleries.
✚ E6 ✉ 1271 Boylston Avenue ☎ 267-8300 or 800 654-2000; fax 267-8300 🚇 Kenmore

SUSSE CHALET

Cheaper option 3 miles south of town. Outdoor pool, bowling alley nearby. Exit 13 off Southeast Expressway.
✚ Off map H10 ✉ 900 Morrissey Boulevard ☎ 287-9200 or 800 258-1980; fax 282-2365 🚇 JFK, then bus or taxi

TREMONT HOUSE

Traditional 1920s hotel right in the Theater District. Chandeliers in the public rooms, modern furnishings in the bedrooms.
✚ G5 ✉ 275 Tremont Street ☎ 426-1400 or 800 331-9998; fax 338-7881 🚇 Boylston

BOSTON INTERNATIONAL YOUTH HOSTEL

Dormitories, cooking facilities available. In summer YHA members only.
✚ E6 ✉ 12 Hemenway Street ☎ 536-9455; fax 424-6558 🚇 Hynes Convention Center

YMCA CENTRAL

The inconvenience of shared bathrooms is offset by maid service. Over 18s only, but no upper age limit.
✚ E6 ✉ 316 Huntington Avenue ☎ 536-7800 🚇 Northeastern

BED & BREAKFAST & SELF-CATERING

There is a shortage of characterful budget-priced hotels in Boston. As a pleasant alternative consider a bed-and-breakfast; many are in very comfortable private homes.

BED & BREAKFAST AGENCY OF BOSTON & BOSTON HARBOR BED & BREAKFAST

A helpful and friendly agency that will find you accommodations in historic houses and restored waterfront lofts. Nightly, weekly, monthly, and winter rates.
✉ 47 Commercial Wharf ☎ 720-3540 or 800 248-9262; fax 523-5761

BOSTON
travel facts

ARRIVING & DEPARTING

When to go

- Boston is pretty in spring but although it is relatively quiet in tourist terms, it is a popular venue for conferences, and hotel space can be snapped up quickly.
- Summer and fall are the peak visiting seasons, with plenty of events and festivals. Hotels are busy around graduation time, and again in October, when Boston serves as a base for trips to see New England's glorious fall foliage.
- The six weeks between Thanksgiving and New Year are another lovely time to visit, with millions of tiny lights in the trees and plenty of seasonal festivities.

Climate

- Spring weather, although unpredictable, can be wonderful, with cool nights and fresh days ranging from 60° to 70°F (April–May).
- Boston enjoys pleasantly warm summers, peaking in July, when the temperatures creep towards 90°F.
- Fall is generally mild, with September temperatures hovering in the upper 60s°F.
- Winters are very cold, with snow often falling between December and February and temperatures around the mid-20s°F.

Arriving by air

- Logan Airport, 3 miles from downtown Boston, has five terminals connected by walkways, free shuttle buses, restaurants, hotels and all the other facilities you would expect of a major international airport.
- Buses marked "Massport" carry passengers free to the Airport T station; from here it's a few minutes' journey to downtown Boston (85¢). The shuttle runs every 8–12 minutes, 5:30AM–1AM.
- An Airport Water Shuttle runs between Logan and Rowes Wharf in the financial district (every 15 minutes Mon–Fri 6AM–8PM; every 30 minutes Fri 8PM–11PM, Sat 10AM–11PM, Sun 10AM–8PM. No service Dec 25, Jan 1, July 4, Thanksgiving Day. $8). It's far and away the most exciting way to arrive in town. An on-call water taxi also runs from the airport ☎ 422-0392.
- Metered taxis are available at all airport terminals (average fare to downtown $10–18). Included in this is the toll the driver pays for using the tunnel under the harbor; you may be handed the receipt.

Arriving by bus

- Greyhound and Peter Pan buses travel frequently between New York and Boston, arriving at the Trailways Terminal, 585 Atlantic Avenue, by South Station.
- Greyhound buses ☎ 800 231-2222.
- Peter Pan buses ☎ 482-6620.

Arriving by car

- From the west, I-90 runs into Boston with Exits 18–20 leading to Cambridge, Exit 22 to Back Bay, Fenway, Kenmore Square and Boston Common, and Exit 24 leading to Downtown and the North and South Highway.
- From the south, State Route 128 east and State Route 9 have exits marked Kneeland Street, Chinatown, and Dock Square (for the airport).

- U.S. 1, I-93 and I-95 lead in from the north with exits marked Storrow Drive (for Cambridge and Boston Common), High Street (for Downtown), and Kneeland Street (for Chinatown and the Theater District).

Arriving by train

- Amtrak (☎ 482-3660) runs almost hourly between Boston and New York, Philadelphia, and Washington, DC, arriving at South Station.
- Train journeys from New York to Boston take between four and five hours.

ESSENTIAL FACTS

Alcohol

- It is illegal to drink alcohol in public places, e.g., the T or the street.

Etiquette

- In restaurants a 5 percent meal tax is added to the bill. A tip of 15–20 percent is usually expected.
- Tip 15 percent for taxis and $1 to $1.50 a bag for airport and hotel porters.
- Some restaurants require jackets and ties for men, but on the whole evening meals are informal affairs.
- In restaurants evening meals are usually served between 6 and 10PM on weekdays, later on weekends.

Insurance

- Travel insurance covering baggage, health, and trip cancellation or interruptions is available from: Access America (Box 90315, Richmond, VA 23286 ☎ 804/285 3300 or 800/284 8300), Carefree Travel Insurance (Box 9366, 100 Garden City Plaza, Garden City, NY 11530 ☎ 516/294 0220 or 800/323 3149)

Near Travel Service (Box 1339, Calumet City, IL 60409, ☎ 708/868 6700 or 800/654 6700) Tele-Trip (Mutual of Omaha Plaza, Box 31716, Omaha, NE 68131 ☎ 800/228 9792) Travel Insured International (Box 280568, East Hartford, CT 06128 0568 ☎ 203/528 7663 or 800/243 3174) Travel Guard International (1145 Clark Street, Stevens Point, WI 54481 ☎ 715/345 0505 or 800/826 1300) Wallach & Company (107 W. Federal Street, Box 480, Middleburg, VA 22117 ☎ 703/687 3166 or 800/237 6615).

Sensible precautions

- When exploring Boston, as any other large city, a few basic precautions are advisable:
- After dark, stick to well-lit and well populated areas. At night, avoid Boston Common and the southern half of Washington Street.
- To be sure of being safe, discuss your itinerary with your hotel's reception staff so they can point out any potential problems.
- Be aware of the people and activities around you, especially at night or in quiet areas.
- Keep your wallet or purse tucked out of sight and don't carry valuables or cash openly. Do not carry easily snatched bags and cameras, or stuff your wallet into your back pocket. In a bar or restaurant, keep your belongings within sight and within reach.
- Keep valuables in the safe of your hotel and never carry any more money than you need. Wads of cash are seldom necessary, and it is safer to make major purchases with traveler's checks or credit cards.

- Lost traveler's checks are relatively quick and easy to replace. Keep the numbers of the checks separate from the checks themselves.
- If only in order to make an insurance claim, you should report any stolen item to the nearest police station. It is highly unlikely that any stolen goods will be recovered, but the police will be able to fill out the forms that your insurance company will need.
- If you use a car, lock the doors and keep bags and valuables out of sight.

Money matters

- Nearly all banks have ATMs. Before leaving home, check which network your cards are linked to and ensure your personal identification number (PIN) is valid.
- For specific Cirrus locations in the United States and Canada, call 800/424 7787.
- For US Plus locations, call 800/843 7587 and enter the area code and first three digits of the number you're calling from (or of the calling area where you want an ATM).

Holidays

- 1 Jan: New Year's Day
  3rd Mon in Jan – Martin Luther King Day
  3rd Mon in Feb – President's Day
  last Mon in May – Memorial Day
  July 4 – Independence Day
  1st Mon in Sep – Labor Day
  2nd Mon in Oct – Columbus Day
  Nov 11 – Veterans Day
  4th Thu in Nov – Thanksgiving Day
  Dec 25 – Christmas Day.

- Boston also celebrates:
  Mar 17 – Evacuation Day;
  3rd Mon in Apr – Patriots Day;
  Jun 17 – Bunker Hill Day

Opening hours

- Banks: Mon–Fri 9–3; Thu 9–5 or later; Sat 9–2.
- Shops: Mon–Sat 10–6 or later. Shops are closed Sun mornings.
- Museums and sights: Mon–Sat 10–5 (or 4 if guided tours given); from noon Sun. Unless otherwise stated, all sights mentioned in this book close on Thanksgiving and Christmas.
- Offices: Mon–Fri 8 or 9–5.

Places of worship

- Congregationalist: Park Street Church ✉ 1 Park Street
- Episcopalian: Trinity Church ✉ Copley Square
- First Baptist Church: ✉ 110 Commonwealth Avenue
- Jewish: contact Religious Information Services ✉ 177 Tremont Street, Boston ☎ 426-2139
- Roman Catholic: St. Stephen's Church ✉ 401 Hanover Street
- Unitarian: Arlington Street Church ✉ 351 Boylston Street

Restrooms

- Public restrooms are few and far between downtown. There are some in the Visitor Center opposite the Old State House in State Street, in Faneuil Hall Marketplace, and on Boston Common.
- Buy a drink before you use the restroom in a bar.
- Best bets: department stores, hotels and, in a pinch, busy restaurants.

Smoking

- Smoking is banned in many places, including the T. Some hotels have no-smoking floors. By law all restaurants have smoke-free areas and some ban smoking altogether.
- Cambridge is by law smoke-free.

Student travelers

- To get discounts on transportation and admissions, get an International Student Identity Card (ISIC) if you're a bona fide student, or the International Youth Card (IYC) if you're under 26. The ISIC and IYC cards cost $16 each and include basic travel accident and illness coverage, plus a toll-free travel hotline. Apply through the Council on International Educational Exchange (CIEE, 205 E. 42nd Street, 16th Floor, New York, NY 10017 ☎ 212/661 1450) and in Boston (729 Boylston Street, Boston, MA 02116 ☎ 617/266 1926). There are also locations in Miami, FL 33156 ☎ 305/670 9261), Los Angeles (1093 Broxton Avenue, Los Angeles, CA 90024 ☎ 310/208 3551), and 43 college towns nationwide.
- Twice a year, the CIEE publishes *Student Travels* magazine. The CIEE's Council Travel Service offers domestic air passes for bargain travel within the U.S. and is the exclusive agent for several student-discount cards.

Tickets

- For tickets for performing arts and sports events, museums and trolley tours see panel ➤ 80.

Time

- Between the first Saturday in April and the last Saturday in

October Massachusetts puts its clocks ahead one hour for Daylight Saving Time.

Tourist offices

- Greater Boston Convention & Visitors Bureau Inc ✉ Prudential Tower, Suite 400, PO Box 490, Boston MA 02199 ☎ 536-4100; fax 424-7664.
- Massachusetts Office of Travel & Tourism ✉ 100 Cambridge Street, Boston MA 02202 ☎ 727-3201; fax 727-6525.
- Boston National Historical Park Visitor Center ✉ 15 State Street, opposite Old State House ☎ 935-3952
- Boston Common Information Kiosk ✉ Tremont Street ☎ 426-3115.
- Cambridge Visitor Information ✉ Harvard Square, Cambridge ☎ 497-1630.

Visitors with disabilities

- Like most major cities, Boston is well equipped for visitors with disabilities. Public buildings, parking lots, and subway stations provide wheelchair access, and some hotels have specially designed rooms.
- Advice and information is available from:
  The Information Center for Individuals with Disabilities ✉ 27–43 Wormwood Street, Boston MA 02210 ☎ 450-9888.

PUBLIC TRANSPORTATION & CAR RENTAL

Subway

- Known simply as the T, the MBTA (Massachusetts Bay Transportation Authority) runs subway and elevated trains along four "rapid transit" lines: Red, Green, Orange and Blue, all of which meet in downtown Boston. The T is clean, efficient, safe, and easy to use. "Inbound" and "Outbound" refer to the direction in relation to Park Street Station.

- Trains run between 5AM (later on Sun) and 12.45AM.
- Tokens (85¢) can be bought at station booths. Buy several at once to save time. One token covers any trip right out to the suburbs, but the journey back can cost more.
- T visitor passports give unlimited travel for one, three, or seven days; available at the Greater Boston Convention & Visitors Bureau and at Park Street Station information booth.
- Free maps of MTBA routes are available at the Park Street Station information booth. Some maps do not show all stops on the Green Line branches.

Buses

- Very few bus routes run into downtown Boston; most visitors find the T quicker and handier.
- Buses travel farther out into the suburbs than the T and are used mainly by commuters.
- Passengers must have the exact change (85¢) or an MTBA token.

Boats

- The airport water shuttle sails regularly across Boston Harbor (► 88 for times).
- Commuter boats are operated by: Mass Bay Lines ✉ 60 Rowes Wharf ☎ 542-8000
  Boston Harbor Commuter Service ✉ 349 Lincoln Street, Hingham ☎ 740-1253.
  For ferry services to Charlestown ► 43.

Car rental

- Driving in Boston is a nightmare. Use public transportation, which is quick, efficient, and avoids any parking problems. A car is useful only for some trips out of Boston.
- Rental drivers must generally be at least 21; many companies put the minimum age at 25 or charge extra for those aged between 21 and 25.
- Never drive after drinking and don't keep opened alcohol in the car. Park only in legal spots or you will be towed.
- There is a 5 percent tax on car rentals.
- Major car rental companies in Boston include:
  Avis ☎ 800 331-1212
  Budget ☎ 800 527-0700
  Dollar ☎ 800 800-4000
  Hertz ☎ 800 654-3131
  National InterRent ☎ 800 227-7368

Taxis

- Taxis can be hailed on the street or found at hotels and taxi stands.
- 24-hour taxi services are run by Checker Cab Co ☎ 497-9000 or 536-7000
  Red & White Cab ☎ 242-8000;
  Bay State Taxi Service ☎ 566-5000
  Independent Taxi Operators Association ☎ 426-7000.

MEDIA & COMMUNICATIONS

Post offices

- Main post offices are situated at:
  Charles Street Station
  Hanover Street Station (north end)
  Faneuil Hall Station

Prudential Center Retail Store, 800 Boylston Street, and Harvard Square Retail Store, 125 Mt. Auburn Street.

Telephones

- The Boston area code is 617. The telephone numbers given in this book do not include this.
- Pay phones take 5¢, 10¢, and 25¢ coins and phone cards, which can be bought in denominations of $5, $10, $20, $50, and $100, and recharged using a credit card.
- Local calls still cost 10¢.

Newspapers

- The newsstand at Harvard Square T station, Cambridge, sells a vast range of newspapers and magazines.
- Two daily newspapers, the *Boston Globe* and the less liberal *Boston Herald*, list cultural and entertainment events – the *Globe* on Thursday, the *Herald* on Friday each week.
- The weekly *Boston Phoenix* also carries a guide to what's on (Saturday).
- The monthly *Boston Magazine* reviews the Boston scene and gives coveted awards to restaurants.

Magazines

- Free tourist-aimed magazines are to be found in hotel lobbies; their discount coupons can save money on sightseeing and food.

EMERGENCIES

Emergency phone numbers

- Police: 911
- 24-hour pharmacy: CVS ✉ Porter Square Shopping Plaza, Cambridge ☎ 247-2768
- Massachusetts General Hospital ☎ 726-2000

Medical treatment

- Boston Evening Medical Center ☎ 267 7171
- Eye and Ear Infirmary ☎ 523-7900
- Physician Referral Service ☎ 726-5800, weekdays 8:30–5
- Dental emergency ☎ 651-3521
- See also Emergency phone numbers, above.

Lost property

- To report lost credit cards: American Express ☎ 800 528-2121
  Diners Club/Carte Blanche ☎ 1/800 234-6377
  MasterCard ☎ 800 826-2181
  Visa ☎ 800 227-6811
- To report lost traveler's checks: American Express ☎ 800 221-7282
  Thomas Cook ☎ 800 223-7373.

INDEX

Citypack
Boston

While every care has been taken to ensure the accuracy of the information in this guide, time brings change, and consequently the publisher cannot accept responsibility for errors that may occur. Prudent travelers will therefore want to call ahead to verify prices and other "perishable" information.

Copyright   © 1997 by The Automobile Association
Maps copyright   © 1997 by The Automobile Association
Fold-out map   © RV Reise- und Verkehrsverlag Munich · Stuttgart
                   © Cartography: GeoData

All rights reserved under International and Pan-American Copyright Conventions. Distributed by Random House, Inc., New York. No maps, illustrations, or other portions of this book may be reproduced in any form without written permission from the publishers.

Published in the United States by Fodor's Travel Publications, Inc.
Published in the United Kingdom by AA Publishing

Fodor's is a registered trademark of Fodor's Travel Publications, Inc.

ISBN 0-679-03425-0

FODOR'S CITYPACK BOSTON

AUTHOR *Sue Gordon*
CARTOGRAPHY *The Automobile Association*
             RV Reise- und Verkehrsverlag
COVER DESIGN *Fabrizio La Rocca, Allison Saltzman*
COPY EDITOR *Sean Connolly*
VERIFIER *Richard Allnatt*
INDEXER *Marie Lorimer*

Acknowledgments

The author would like to thank the following for their assistance in preparing this book: British Airways, Greater Boston Convention & Visitors Bureau, Sarah Mann and Hope Thurlby of Discover New England, and Ferne Mintz of Bed & Breakfast Agency of Boston.
The Automobile Association wishes to thank the following photographers, libraries and associations in the preparation of this book:
Boston Athenaeum 39 (Photograph by Peter Vanderwarker. Collection of the Boston Athenaeum); The Bridgeman Art Library 28b *Long Branch* (detail) by Winslow Homer (1836–1910) Museum of Fine Arts, Boston Massachusetts; Computer Museum 47 (Fayfoto); Mary Evans Picture Library 12; S. Gordon 45a, 51; Harvard University Art Museums 26a (Courtesy of the Fogg Art Museum), 26b Gift of Paul J. Sachs in honour of Edward W. Forbe's thirtieth year as Director of the Fogg Museum); R.Holmes 25a, 44a; John F. Kennedy Library & Museum 48b (Robert Schoen); New England Aquarium 46a, 46b; Old South Meeting House 40a; Old Town Trolley Tours 19;
All remaining pictures are held in the Association's own Library (AA Photo Library) and were taken by Clive Sawyer with the exception of the following: R. Holmes, 5b, 13a, 22a, 33b, 36b, 40b, 45b, 49b, 52b, 61a, 87a, 87b; M. Lynch 1, 24b, 25b, 36a, 60, 61b;

Special sales

Fodor's Travel Publications are available at special discounts for bulk purchases (100 copies or more) for sales promotions or premiums. Special editions, including personalized covers, excerpts of existing guides, and corporate imprints, can be created in large quantities for special needs. For more information write to Special Marketing, Fodor's Travel Publications, 201 East 50th St., New York NY 10022.

Color separation by Daylight Colour Art Pte Ltd, Singapore
Manufactured by Dai Nippon Printing Co. (Hong Kong) Ltd
10 9 8 7 6 5 4 3 2 1

Titles in the Citypack series

• Amsterdam • Atlanta • Berlin • Boston• Chicago • Florence • Hong Kong •
• London • Los Angeles • Miami • Montréal • New York • Paris • Prague •
• Rome • San Francisco • Sydney • Tokyo • Toronto • Venice • Washington, D.C.